You Want to Be
A
Life Coach

Special message to you. Turn the page →

Anthology

By
Coach J Dianne Tribble

&

Coaches At the Table:
Gigi Blackshear, Ronline Cannady,
Cindy Coates, Gina Jackson, Alvin W. King,
Shara Mondy, & Iris T. Moore

At the Table
Life Coaching & Motivational Speaking Services
Unveiling Your Full Potential

COPYRIGHT

ISBN-13: 978-1506025810

ISBN-10: 1506025811

Printed in the United States of America
First Edition

At the Table
Life Coaching & Motivational Speaking Services
Unveiling Your Full Potential

Cover created by: Antar Austin, Art Director

To My Dear Friend,
Miss Judy Johnson

— I thank GOD upon every
remembrance of you. You
have been a joy and faithful
friend ever since we connected.
Your beautiful positive spirit is
so contagious. May this book

Anthology - a book or other collection of
selected writings by various authors, usually
in the same literary form, of the same period,
or on the same subject: ~ Dictionary.com

bless
you
and
encourage you.
Enjoy. Enjoy. Enjoy.
— I love you my Sister.
May GOD continuously bless
and keep you.
Joy & Peace,
JD Dianne Dibble

2-11-2015

Smile,
you're loved.

~ Coach J Dianne Tribble

Assisting my clients in connecting with their motivation

Endorsements

So You Want to Be a Life Coach gives an excellent and thorough look into every aspect of the Coaching profession. The authors present you with a practical and personal look into the life of a Coach that will aid you in your quest to become a Life Coach. As a coach for the past ten years, I would encourage you to dive into this book wholeheartedly and digest every helpful nugget it provides. What a dynamic resource this is to the fabulous and rewarding field of coaching.
Tanya Stewart, Wife Coach & Founder of Spirit Filled Wives

Wow! If you ever need to understand the purpose of a life coach, this is a must read. I found myself not only captivated by the personal testimonies of each coach, but the most impressive highlight of this book for me is the variety of step-by-step life skill activities unique to each coach intertwined and connected to their story which says "this is real!". This book in one word...Engaging!
Dianne E. Woods, Founder, DEW Ministries, Jacksonville, FL.

"So You Want to be A Life Coach Anthology" is a "must read" for persons whose talent is the gift of helping! Social Workers could benefit from this easy read, as well as ministry workers, such as myself. In this anthology, it characterizes many social work values and beliefs. The definition of "being present in the moment" is so important... for those of us who want to help move people forward from mundane to extraordinary. Coach J. Dianne Tribble and the coaches she has trained, are certainly helping people to transition into "The Star" that lies within us. I enthusiastically endorse this book to all who believe "...if we sit here...we die here."
Stephanie Parr, Former Program Coordinator, The Community Church. Lake Station, IN

About the Cover

The puzzle pattern was selected because as Life Coaches, we major in assisting our Clients in connecting to their motivation. While the majority of the puzzle is **green**, there are three pieces featured in **red**, **yellow**, and **purple**. These colors signify two things:

1. There are times in life when we sense a void. There is something missing. Sometimes we know exactly what it is and at other times, we don't. Soliciting the help of a Life Coach could prove most beneficial in identifying "it" and developing a plan to implement "it."

2. The colors are significate to the overall heart of At the Table Life Coaching & Motivational Speaking Services LLC.

   Green – represents growth, health, wisdom, insight, fertility, renewal, and revelation.

   Red – represents the love and passion for working with people and seeing them win at life.

   Yellow – represents the trust factor, safety, unity, joy, peace, and optimism.

   Purple – represents royalty. You are somebody. You are special. And you are important.

Dedication:

<u>So You Want to Be A Life Coach Anthology</u> is dedicated to my family and the family members of all the contributing authors. We love and appreciate you all. Thank you for believing in us.

And we know that all things work together for good to them that love God, to them who are the called according to His purpose. ~ Romans 8:28

TABLE OF CONTENTS

Acknowledgements

It gives me great honor to acknowledge the following people for their support and belief in me, and in the promotion of this project:

- ❖ Thank you first and foremost to my **Heavenly Father** for blessing me with another literary work. I am honored and humbled.
- ❖ **Larry Tribble**, my beloved husband – Thank you for believing in me and encouraging me to move forward with this project. Thank you for releasing me to follow my heart. Any success I could possibly gain, has your name on it as well because I could not do the things in which I do without your support. Thank you Love.
- ❖ **Ebony, Erika, & Andre Tribble,** my beloved children – Thank you for your support in word and deed as you have helped me with the marketing, promotional, and technological support. **Erika**, thank you for your assistance with the book lay-out. We did it!
- ❖ **Contributing authors** – Thank you to the following Coaches for joining me in this project: Gigi Blackshear, Ronline Cannady, Cindy Coates, Gina Jackson, Alvin W. King, Shara Mondy, & Iris T. Moore. What a great team! Thank you!
- ❖ **To all Coaches At the Table** – Thank you all for being the great community of professional Life Coaches in which you are. Thank you for your support and dedication.
- ❖ **Antar Austin,** creative art director – Thank you for capturing the heart of the book by designing an outstanding cover!
- ❖ **Paula Scruggs,** hair designer & confidante – Thank you for your support and encouragement. I appreciate you!

- ❖ **We Are Women In Business** – Thank you to my professional business group Sisters for your heart-felt support in the promotion of this project. I am extremely proud to say "group elevation" causes us all to win. Quen, I could not imagine a better co-leader. Love you!

- ❖ **Coach's Café and Coach Jacksonville** – Thank you to my coaching support groups. Each time I attend the meetings, I leave challenged and encouraged, knowing I have invested in myself by spending quality time with my fellow-coaches.

- ❖ **E3 Business Group** – Thank you Mr. Butler for your role in inspiring the title of the anthology based on your signature class, "So You Want to Be an Entrepreneur." Best wishes.

- ❖ **Family, Friends and Connections** – Thank you to my extended family, dear friends, and all my social media connections who have faithfully followed me and the business/ministry, At the Table Life Coaching & Motivational Speaking Services LLC. Your connections, "Likes," and comments have provided encouragement as I continuously work to fulfill my purpose and grow the business ministry.

- ❖ **Pamela James presents Ladies Night Out** – Thank you for your faithful support and open platform to share my gifts and talents. I call you friend through thick and thin. Here's to your continuous success! I believe in you.

- ❖ **Bishop George & Pastor April Davis** – As you have faithfully taught us the Word over the years, it has supplied me with the ultimate support, encouragement, and energy to fulfill my God given purpose. Thank you. Larry & I love you both for Life.

Introduction

Are you an exhorter or encourager? Do you enjoy seeing people win? Are you passionate about helping others? Do you have a good listening ear?

As one of the fastest growing industries in the world today, Life Coaching has also become one of the top "buzz words." By sharing our stories, it is our desire that you will walk away with not only an accurate understanding of Life Coaching, but will also be able to determine whether pursuing a certification within this field is right for you.

Reflecting back to 2009 when I was initially introduced to Life Coaching, I not only wanted to obtain my certification, I also wanted everyone to know that help is out there and available to assist you in obtaining your dreams, hopes, and desires. You don't have to do it alone. I wanted people to know that they could increase the likelihood of conquering goals by partnering with a Life Coach.

With a strong background in employee development and training, I knew that I would one day write my own certification program. After dedicating almost a year in development and implementation, I rolled the program out in March of 2012. The program has proven to be a great success, producing new Professional Certified Life Coaches locally, nationally, and internationally. We're simply helping people win at life.

After coaching numerous Clients and training nearly 60 new Life Coaches over the past six years, I have witnessed so many success stories. The successes serve as motivating fuel to keep me moving forward in assisting others in winning.

I was blessed to connect a group of fellow- Life Coaches who were willing to join me in this project. Through our shared stories, may you be motivated to get up, get busy, and win! People are awaiting your obedience. Enjoy!

~ Coach J Dianne Tribble

~Our Stories~

~ *Life Story One* ~

Coach J Dianne Tribble

CEO & founder of At the Table Life Coaching & Motivational Speaking Services LLC. She is a Professional Christian Life Coach/Trainer, motivational speaker, and published author. She is the founder of her company's Life Coach Certification program which has produced more than 55 Professional Life Coaches to date. Active in the community, she is a member of Impact Church, under the leadership of Bishop George & Pastor April Davis, where she serves faithfully in the Ministry of Helps Department. She is the Volunteer Liaison for Junior Achievement North Florida; an ambassador for PACE Center for Girls; facilitator and tutor for Duval County Schools; member of PUSH Women's Ministries; and co-founder of We Are Women in Business, a professional women's support group. She is a strong advocate of group elevation (cooperative economics). She is the author of the life-inspiring book, The Star Inside of You Motivational Nuggets & Inspirational Stories of Encouragement. She has been a regularly featured writer for Entrepreneurs Anchor Magazine and eZine Articles. Married 33 years to her best friend, Larry, they are the parents of three successful adult children.

Meet Me At the Table

I'm J Dianne Tribble, founder and CEO of At the Table Life Coaching & Motivational Speaking Services LLC. Come join me At the Table as I share my story. Here we are. What a beautiful green tabletop. This represents a place of growth, wisdom, insight, and revelation. Three exquisite candles strategically placed make up the stunning centerpiece. The purple candle represents royalty. You are somebody. You are special. The yellow candle makes me smile. It symbolizes our unity, fellowship, and a safe environment to share from the heart. There's also the captivating red candle. It represents the commitment, passion, and love in which I have for what I am called to do.

At my table, your drink awaits you. It will provide soothing refreshment as you relax and center on the quality time we will share. The ambience is so inviting. The appetizer warms you up in preparation for the main course. While I can assure you the appetizer will be good, it is only a for-taste of the delightful meal to come.

As you partake, endorphins are released as you smile, laugh, and allow yourself to enjoy the moment. This is followed by the awaited main course. It has been beautifully prepared, well balanced with meat, vegetables, and bread. Delicious! Would you like some dessert? I'll leave that up to you. With it or without it, your experience At the Table will be robust, filling, and memorable.

For I know the thoughts that I think toward you, says the LORD,
thoughts of peace, and not of evil, to give you an expected end.
~ Jeremiah 29:11

This scripture is very near and dear to me. Experiences throughout my life prepared me to launch At the Table. As a young child in elementary school, I loved to write and present my written stories in our local 4-H Club public speaking contests. Shaking and frightened, I rose above my fears, presented my speeches, and took home several blue ribbons. You know the ones that turn purple.

In middle school, I began to journal. Writing was my escape. It was the place I could express my most embarrassing and difficult times, as well as the happiest moments of my life. Writing brought some measure of sense to non-sense and things I clearly did not understand. I continued to journal off and on throughout my high school years.

Journaling became a permanent fixture back in 1982 after I married my beloved husband, Larry. As a new recruit in the Navy, he encouraged me to write while he was away on deployments. This helped me and it helped him to understand the life of his Navy wife.

I was a stay-home mom for the first 15 years of our marriage as we raised our three children; however, I was active in the community. I was a faithful volunteer and PTA member of the children's schools. I was active in our churches as a Sunday school teacher, Bible study leader, worship leader, and women's group leader.

Big on education, I participated in several training programs and courses as our family moved from duty station to duty station. After all our children left the nest, I went back to college, earning my Bachelors' degree in Business Management. I also completed a two-year Layman's Bible School training program from my local church, Impact Church (Pastors George & April Davis).

I joined the fulltime workforce officially in 1996, quickly scaling the ladder of success. I entered the doors of Corporate America in an entry-level position. My leadership, interpersonal, and business organization skills were quickly recognized and utilized. Promotions positioning me to manage work groups quickly followed.

Following my heart's desire, in 2008 I founded and hosted a successful women's support group forum in Corporate America. The success of the forum expanded to include quarterly community forums as well. The presentations were always followed by open discussions, which encouraged the participants to actively participate.

In 2009, I had lunch with a friend who had recently retired several months earlier. As we laughed and spent time catching up with each other, she shared the fact that she had recently completed a Life Coaching certification program. This marked my initial introduction to Life Coaching. I asked for details. As she shared, I realized I had been doing a form of Life Coaching for years without knowing such a career field existed.

After discussing the certification program with my husband, I completed detailed research on my own. I found a program in which I was interested in and aggressively pursued the program. Upon completing the coaching certification and training process, I knew in my heart I was ready to launch the business and that I would one day write my own certification program.

To keep my skills sharp, I consistently coached at least two clients on a regular basis, as I also maintained my management position in Corporate America. I soon discovered, this worked in my favor. My coaching skills were sharpened as a result of consistently practicing the skills.

In 2011, I left Corporate America to aggressively pursue my small business dream. One of my initial goals, was to keep my word in which I had spoken two years prior by writing my own Life Coaching certification program. I worked on the project for approximately 10 months. I rolled the program out to the public during the spring of 2012, with three initial trainees. These three trainees were very instrumental in assisting me in tweaking and fine-tuning the program.

To date, At the Table Life Coaching & Motivational Speaking Services LLC has produced almost 60 Certified Professional Christian Life Coaches. They are located across the United States, as well as internationally in Abu Dhabi, United Arab Emirates.

To neglect your passion, is like neglecting one of the most exquisite and expensive gifts you could ever receive. ~ Coach J Dianne Tribble

What Is Life Coaching?

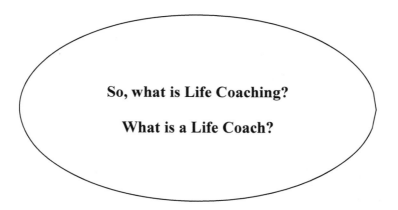

So, what is Life Coaching?

What is a Life Coach?

There is no one set definition for Life Coaching. Therefore, I will share with you a few of my definitions:

1. Life Coaching is partnering in a relationship with a person, in which we refer to as a Client, to assist him or her in setting goals, putting a strategic plan in place to realize the goal, and seeing the goal come to fruition.

2. Life Coaching is a support system for change in an individual's life.

3. Life Coaching is a transforming relationship which is client-centered as the Coach assist the Client in unveiling his or her potential.

4. Life Coaching is the process of a Coach intuitively listening as a Client shares from the heart. The Coach ask good quality questions as a result, which encourages the Client to think through the response. Doable actions steps are considered and put in place. The Coach, as a support structure, holds the Client accountable for fulfilling the action steps.

5. Life Coaching is simply helping people win in life by believing in them, holding them accountable, and sticking with them through thick and thin to see the dreams, desires, and aspirations come to pass.

6. Life Coaching is hiring your own personal cheerleader to affirm you in navigating the course to living your dreams.

What Is a Life Coach?

A Life Coach is the professional business title earned and given to the person providing Life Coaching services to Clients. A Life Coach is a "change agent" in assisting individuals to make the necessary changes in their lives, in order to live their dreams or to obtain their goals.

What Are the Benefits of Working with a Life Coach?

- ❖ You will have your own personal cheerleader.
- ❖ Your chances of reaching personal goals and successfully making life changes greatly increase.
- ❖ You don't have to do "it" alone.
- ❖ Your confidence will increase if you are committed to the process.
- ❖ The safe environment fosters authenticity.
- ❖ The process challenges you to think, and generate options and solutions on your own with the guidance of the Coach.
- ❖ It's an investment in personal development.
- ❖ You get to talk about what you want to talk about. The process is all about "you."
- ❖ Fear of the unknown is normally minimized or eliminated by having a support structure (your Life Coach) in place.

Reflections...

Notes...

Capturing my thoughts:

_____

_____

_____

_____

_____

_____

Life Coach Assessment

Consider your responses to the following assessment to help determine if you would be a good fit as a Life Coach. Please answer "yes" or "no."

1. _____ I am a motivator, encourager, exhorter, or cheerleader.

2. _____ I enjoy assisting others in making and reaching goals.

3. _____ People value what I have to say.

4. _____ I exercise good listening skills which help to unveil the bottom line.

5. _____ I am a leader.

6. _____ I am an extrovert.

7. _____ I am tactful in telling people when I know or feel they are wrong.

8. _____ I enjoy seeing people win.

9. _____ I am warm and friendly.

10. _____ I am patient and considerate.

11. _____ I believe in people.

12. _____ People are drawn to me.

If your responses included 10-12 "yes" responses, you are an ideal candidate for a Life Coach. If you scored 8-9 "yes" responses, proactive research and continuing education may help prepare you to become a Life Coach. Submitting to personal Life Coaching for yourself may also prove to be beneficial. Retake the assessment after taking these proactive steps. A score of 6-7 indicates more extensive research, education, interpersonal skill building, and self-improvement are required prior to pursuing a career in Life Coaching. A score of 5 or less indicates the need for personal reconsideration in pursuing this field. Consider investing in yourself by hiring a personal Life Coach for self-improvement.

What action steps are you motivated to take as a result of this assessment?

Action steps:
_____
_____
_____
_____

Connecting with Your Motivation

In order for a coaching relationship to be truly effective, the Life Coach must successfully connect the Client to his/her motivation. What does this mean? This means that once the Client identifies the goal he/she would like to work towards, creating a visual of the end product is used to assist the Client in the progressive process of bringing the goal to fruition.

This is accomplished by:

1. Asking the Client to create a mental picture and share it with the Coach.
2. Having the Client create a vision board of the end-product.
3. Requesting the Client journal the journey.

~ *Coach J Dianne Tribble*

It's Time to Get Present in the Moment

By: Coach J Dianne Tribble

We often hear the expression or maybe you have used it yourself, "Where did the time go?" Life in general seems to present so many demands on our most precious commodity. This precious commodity is commonly known as our time. Our time stands still for no one. Life pulls on our time from every angle. Effective management of our time requires getting present in the moment and resting there. Successfully reaching this point usually produces peace, productivity, and contentment among many other benefits.

What does it mean to "get present in the moment?" Getting present in the moment is an expression for getting grounded in the present (here and now), free of the pressures and demands of regret and anxiety. "Getting present in the moment" refers to coming face-to-face with where you are right now in your life; embracing that place; and resting in that place. I would venture further to state that it is about confidently operating moment by moment in life as it unfolds.

To visually explain the phrase "getting present in the moment," imagine standing up and looking down at your feet. Image both feet together side-by-side, with your toes aligned straight ahead of you. This position represents being "present in the moment." Both feet are planted confidently side by side. In this position, an individual is able to effectively respond to daily demands, challenges, and triumphs, free of stress. With toes pointed ahead, this position encourages forward momentum and progress.

Operating in the moment can be a great challenge for some people. Instead of finding both feet firmly and confidently planted side-by-side, one foot can be found several inches behind the other. This position denotes regret. In other words, a person postured in this position tends to revert back to pass failures and short comings. The voice of disappointing attempts hinders this person from confidently moving ahead. The voice of regret whispers or screams such things as, "Get ready to flop again! Do you recall what happened last time you tried this? Are you sure you want to try this again?"

Not only are the voices of defeat at work when regret is in full force, in addition, the stance of one foot firmly planted while the other foot is behind is a picture of possible retreat. This stance denotes the strong possibility of giving up and turning back. Should the head follow the foot, which is behind, chances of defeat and setbacks greatly increase.

Regret will tend to harass you until you make up your mind to either ignore its voice or you break out with positive affirmations, which will drive the voice of regret to silence. At this point, the foot which lagged behind can be planted firmly in proper position next to the other. Regret works like a smoke screen. While regret whispers or screams discouragement, your confident foot cheers your other foot, which is temporarily arrested by regret, to "Come on and get in agreement with me!"

Another hindrance to "getting present in the moment" is anxiety. While regret, when entertained, causes a person to look back, anxiety works in the opposite direction. It tends to cause one to get ahead of himself or herself. It is driven by the unknown "what ifs." The voice of anxiety will ask nagging and harassing questions such as, "What if it doesn't work out? What will they think? What if you don't do well? What if you don't have enough money?" The questions can be endless and exhausting!

As with regret, the voice of anxiety can be put to silence also. How? Anxiety can be put to silence by the victim making a quality decision to either ignore the voice of anxiety or break out with positive affirmations. One or both of these actions will generally drive the voice of anxiety to silence.

At this point, the foot which raced ahead, can be planted firmly in proper position next to the other. Similar to regret, anxiety works like a smoke screen also. While anxiety whispers or screams unjustified cautions in moving ahead, your confident foot cheers and encourages the foot of anxiety to "Come on and get in agreement with me!"

"Getting present in the moment" is a choice. It can be done. When this choice is made, the individual stands as a victor. A victim would be the result of succumbing to regret and anxiety. Becoming a victim is a choice as well.

There are numerous benefits to "getting present in the moment." These benefits include:

- **Increased confidence** – This would be belief in yourself and the personal ability to do whatever you must do or you are challenged to do. There is no room for fear and second-guessing.

- **Increased chances of success** – When fear is mastered, the chances of success automatically increase. There is the possibility that things will not work out. If so, just be willing to try it again.

- **Optimism** – A positive attitude and outlook go a long way. When you believe in yourself and your ability to succeed, you increase the chances of experiencing success.

- **Peace and tranquility** – When the quality decision is made to "get present in the moment," it produces peace and tranquility. You can rest in your decision and proceed ahead.

- **Increased value** – The quality decision to "get present in the moment" is evidence that what you are facing and your desired results are important to you. "Getting present in the moment" adds value to your desires.

- **Open doors of opportunity** – "Getting present in the moment" is the willful choice to walk through the smoke screens of life. When you do so, doors of new opportunity are subject to open.

Life will continue to pull on your time. To manage the pulls, be willing to allow yourself to "get present in the moment." The benefits far outweigh the results of regret and anxiety. Get both feet firmly planted in front of you and "walk on." You can do it. Here's to your continuous success!

~ Coach J Dianne Tribble

My Favorites

Scripture

"And this is the confidence that we have in him, that, if we ask any thing according to his will, he heareth us: And if we know that he hear us, whatsoever we ask, we know that we have the petitions that we desired of him.
~ I John 5:14,15

Quote

"You can have everything in life you want, if you'll just help enough people get what they want."
~ Zig Ziglar

Personal Quote

Stay on top of things so things will not be found on top of you. ~ Coach J Dianne Tribble

Favorite Poems

1. "The Road Not Taken" by Robert Frost
2. "Our Deepest Fear" by Marianne Williamson

~ Coach J Dianne Tribble

Top Recommended Reading List

1. <u>Holy Bible</u>

2. <u>The Star Inside of You Motivational Nuggets & Inspirational Stories of Encouragement</u> by J Dianne Tribble (2013)

3. <u>Passing the Tests of Life</u> by George L. Davis (2012)

4. <u>Three Feet from Gold by</u> Sharon L. Lechter & Greg S. Reid (2009)

5. <u>"Make Today Count"</u> by John C. Maxwell (2004)

6. <u>Who Moved My Cheese?</u> by Spencer Johnson, M.D. (1998)

Coach J Dianne Tribble's Contact Information:
At the Table Life Coaching & Motivational Speaking Services LLC
Business Line: (904) 613-8437 Fax Number: (904) 830-0603 Email: coaching@atthetableinc.com LinkedIn.com/in/jdiannetribble Twitter: @AttheTable_wDi Facebook: https://www.facebook.com/jdianne.tribble Facebook Fanpage: https://www.facebook.com/AttheTableLifeCoaching
Always be ready to invest in you!

Testimonials

Coach Tribble is an amazing person who is very passionate about life coaching. I have learned so much from her in our life coaching sessions in handling different situations in life. She holds you accountable for your actions and choices. I admired that about her. She is a person of her word. Coach Tribble is not only my coach, but I consider her to be my sister. I am so grateful to her and her obedience to do and be the person God has called her to be. She not only leads by example, but she is a living example of a true virtuous woman. When I was going through my life coaching certification program, the words that consumed my mind, "She is a wonderful blessing to me. I am so honored to know her and that our paths have crossed." Coach Tribble gives so much of herself to the wonderful world of life coaches. She is my coach for life.   ~ **Lakeisha Williams, Certified Life Coach**

Ms. J. Dianne Tribble was the invited Guest Speaker at the Christ Episcopal Church's Savvy Job Hunters Ministry workshop on July 24, 2014. For two hours, she held the attention of the entire audience by her professional presentation. Ms. Tribble spoke on "The Essential 'C' Experience" which she artfully defined as seven key 'C' areas of success--Change, Confidence, Centered, Consistency, Commercial, Connectors and Celebration. Her analysis was thoughtful, incisive and entertaining. The audience consisted of unemployed job seekers, of all ages, looking for job preparation guidance, as well as motivation and emotional support during this very stressful stage of their lives. Her interactive presentation style was very empathetic, upbeat and positive. She immediately captured everyone's attention and held their interest. Here are some of the audiences' written comments:

"Very inspirational in motivating and defining myself in this transition."

"The instructor is dynamic and really makes you believe in yourself."

"Very enjoyable session. The presenter did an excellent job of showing how the seven 'C's interact with each other and us as individuals."

"Inspiring. I appreciated the upbeat atmosphere." Thorough, concise and pertinent. Very helpful and upbeat".

Ms. Tribble's objective was to provide hope, and breathe life back into the job seekers' dreams, desires and passions. I believe she did accomplished that, and did it in a very receptive manner.

I would certainly recommend Ms. Tribble as a motivational speaker, and look forward to having her as our guest speaker again.

~ Pam Ottesen, Savvy Job Hunters Ministry Leader

Ms. Tribble is a colleague and personal friend I have known for approximately 10 years. Because of her professionalism, passion and enthusiasm for her business and her clients, she was chosen to speak to my Marketing class earlier this year at Jones College. The students loved her presentation and indicated as much in their evaluations. She has been invited again to speak to my Business Communication class in November at Virginia College. Ms. Tribble is a dynamic Motivational Speaker who captivates an audience with her confidence, poise, leadership skills and ability to connect with them. I highly recommend Ms. Tribble for any Public Speaking engagements. **~ Professor Jan Heath, MBA**

Inspiration, Breaking Chains, walking into my Destiny" these are the words that come to mind when I think of my Life coaching session with my Life Coach Dianne Tribble "Coach J". My sessions with Coach J are about glorifying the Father and pulling out of me the greatest that our heavenly Father has put inside of me. I am so grateful to Coach J and our time together. The first words she spoke into my life - Zechariah 4:10 "For who hath despised the day of small things? for these seven shall rejoice, and shall see the plummet in the hand of Zerubbabel. Amen and Thank you Coach J.

~ Zendra Hansley, Client

With a strong desire to see women and men thrive in their purposes, we are committed to the process of assisting our clients to "unveil their full potential" through encouragement, support, partnership, and the application of practical tools.

*~ **At the Table Life Coaching & Motivational Speaking Services LLC Mission Statement***

~ Life Story Two ~

Coach Iris T. Moore

CEO & Founder of CoachEyeMore, L.L.C.

Driven to provide praise and encouragement to the human spirit, Coach Iris T. Moore has traversed corporate America, obtaining over 32 years of influence, impact and leadership skills. She invests her time in transforming lives through CoachEyeMore, L.L.C.; serving as board member of the non-profit organization, The AnnieRuth Foundation; and devotion to her loving spouse of 34 years. Coach Iris' website is coacheyemore.com and email is **transform@coacheyemore.com** *"where transformation is just around the corner."*

"1-800–Displaced…How an Unfortunate Event Captured the True Passion Within Me."

Coach Iris T. Moore

How would you define your "dream Job?"

I have asked that question of many over the years and while the themes of   defining dream jobs differ, reactions to the question rarely does. I mean, have you ever watched the person who shares with you the definition of their dream job? What do you see?

DO you see how their whole countenance change right before your eyes? At times, it is the tension in their face that suddenly goes slack as though someone said to every facial muscle 'its' time to take a nap." Their eyes change, too, as they become glassy and seem to be looking at everything, yet nothing at all. And, their voice is filled with a glow, a light in which dreams shine. Because dreams have a way of transporting people to the highway of "what they want and what they can become." That power emitted from a dream can alter energy so the end result is the manifestation of the dream.

Better yet, is the person who answers your question with, "I am working at my dream job right now." For me, I knew what my dream job was six months after I had joined a fortune 100 Company. It would take another five years before I clinched it.

As long as I can remember, I defined my "dream job" as helping people. The oldest of four siblings and the only girl, I took like a duck to water helping my brothers as they navigated through childhood. The oldest of fifteen grandchildren, I blazed new frontiers only to take copious, mental notes to help guide those who would walk in my shoes. For me, the need and desire to help was ever present and ever right.

My dream job was my role as a Field Sales Manager for a fortune 100 Company. I was entrusted with a team of ten. Each was assigned his or her own geographical territory Field Sales Representatives who worked outside of the great state of Florida. Our company was a household name, so representing a trusted line of branded products to healthcare professionals was a source of pride and personal ownership. I was helping people help people, so it fit my theme as my "dream job." Did it matter that I had to seek three promotions to secure this position? No, because, as I donned my new dream job persona, I was feeling good and purposeful.

You know the feeling I'm talking about. That type of feeling when your first, middle and last name is *GRATITUDE*! When your stride is unwavering, your smile is wide and your outlook is abundant. That is where my head danced as I went to work every day.

Yet, as a new millennium was settling in, so was a wave of uncertainty as word spread of a competitive company who "displaced" 1500 Sales Representatives in one day! As our brands matured, demand waned and our company responded with heroic efforts to retain employees through restructure of the sales-force.

Called Terr-align (I know…sounds scary doesn't it) the process was to redesign Territories by productivity. Because my team had a history of high productivity, minimal change to my Team occurred. Therefore, it was business as usual.

But, that was about to change!

The recession brought a major downsizing to my company in 2009. The uncertainty began as a whisper. Within a week, what followed were anxious calls from my team all asking, "Am I going to have a job?" And, because management did not know, there was little I could do to relieve the fears of my own, loyal and productive Team. And then it came. Directives from the corporate office – management was to inform teams of one thing and one thing only. *Be sure to read the BLAST EMAIL that will come from corporate.* Saddled with this information, I told my team to call the 1-800 number. Little did I know there were two versions of the Blast Emails selectively sent within the company containing two different 1-800 numbers. One number informed you that you had a job and the other number informed you that you were "displaced."

Over the next three days, amidst tearful goodbyes to long time Sales Representatives and preparing reference letters, I was hastily introduced to my new team to manage. As I began the task of building a productive team, I really struggled with several of my new sales representatives. It was painful. It seemed that everything I tried, failed and my joy of managing was dwindling. My dream job conflicted with what I was now doing every day. Have you ever felt that way? You throw everything but the kitchen sink at the problem but nothing seems to work? And, hopelessness begins to set in as you search desperately for solutions.

So, I sought my manager's assistance. He engaged me by asking questions that uncovered "how" I defined the problems. He coached me on how to achieve success with my new representatives. Eager to depart from the feeling of despair, I stopped managing and started "coaching" my team. As a result, not only did those representatives achieve success, they began to refer to me as "Coach." Just as important, our new team achieved success and I regained my passion for my dream job.

Something else happened to me during that time. It was the realization that the new shift to coaching felt like a duck to water! In fact, it felt better than managing because it complemented my keen observation and listening skills. Skills I used since a child were both relevant and valued to meet the needs of my team. I became a natural in recognizing and enhancing the strengths of others.

I achieved my certification as Engagement Coach, read books to advance and my manager recognizing my inherent passion, appointed me as a regional coach to train other managers. Managers sought me out when they had coaching issues. When I asked my peers, "What one thing did I do for them that really helped?" they replied, that my talent was to hyper-focus on what and how they were defining the issue. This generated dialogue that paved the way to hammering out solutions. The most rewarding validation came when I retired. Feeling grateful for the impact I made, acknowledged by my team, I humbly accepted the plaque they presented to me entitled "Circle of Friends." With that vote of confidence, I pursued my certification in Life Coaching to continue my passion of teaming with people to help realize their dreams.

So, what did I learn during one of the most challenging times in my professional life?

I learned that dreams do come true and that they can be lost in a blink of an eye. I learned that seeking assistance can help you regain that dream and it can be better than ever! I also learned that often, the answer to realizing our dreams, lies within us - just out of reach. Why, then, might you ask is the answer *so* hard to grasp?

Well, if you are busy as most, running a hundred miles an hour (I think they call it multi-tasking), it is easy to miss the tiny sprout along the side of the road. Yet, that tiny sprout is often how a solution, a dream or a goal begins as a tiny sprout in the highway of your imagination. I learned, a Life Coach serves as highway signs, prompting you to "slow down" because it is time for introspection, "proceed with caution" as you try on new skillsets and "maintain your speed" once you have course corrected and begin building your path of success. A Life Coach gives you the support to do it "your way" so you obtain the results you want.

Everyone has a Divine design for life. I am *GRATEFUL* every day that my design is in Life Coaching. As a Life Coach my task is to *help* you reveal what your design is, whether it is currently an aspiration, a reality, or a lost or disconnected dream, one question at a time. I couple that with supporting your effort in trekking toward your goal. And, with success in hand, your stride becomes unwavering, your smile becomes wide, and your outlook becomes abundant. Your "new suit of success" suits you because it is YOU! *So, are you ready to "change your lens and change your life"?*

"How to Quell the Ill Wind of Procrastination!"

By Coach Iris T. Moore

Having to shed baggage can be painful.

Recently, I downsized from a big to a small house. Preparing for the move is when the *"ill wind of procrastination"* blew through my home. At times, I felt like an emotional punching bag, hit with memories good and bad. But, I stuck in there. I took that trip down memory lane donating items that others could use, tossing items that had outgrown their purpose and I feel lighter and better for it. *"When you face the tough stuff, the pain has an expiration date!"* I claimed my peace of mind and you can claim yours too!

What is procrastination and more importantly, why do ~90% of us procrastinate at times?

It is defined as avoiding making decisions or completing tasks for which there has been a commitment. So, why do we procrastinate? What fuels indecision and reluctance to "get it done" when you know you committed to doing it?

Human nature fuels what can be referred as the "grandparent" of procrastination. To illustrate this, I want to transport you to the Serengeti, a plain in Northwest Tanzania. Here, we observe the mother lion on the hunt. To feed her cubs, she is engaged in "intense, short term, sustained focus" enabling her to catch her prey and bring food to her cubs. The high level of energy the mother lion expends to complete her task cannot be sustained nor was it intended. That is why after "dinner has been served," a time of playful grooming and sun-baking known as "distractibility" follow, allowing the mother lion to recharge and restore.

Human nature is similar in that it dictates both <u>focus </u>(flight or fight mode) and <u>distractibility</u> as highly useful traits as we navigate through life. Bottom-line is we are hard wired to have varying degrees of both for good reason. That is why we identify with experiencing bouts of procrastination - the opposite of focus. About 25% of us identify ourselves as chronic offenders, constantly procrastinating in every area of our life. What is intended as restorative can linger like an *"ill wind"* and can "blow" us off-course.

The two basic types of procrastination that can "blow" you off-course:

- Deliberate procrastination – "I am waiting till Thursday to do the task because it is not due till Friday." Working better "under pressure" seldom works well because lack of completing the task or compromise of the outcome can result.

- Productive procrastination – This is insidious because while many tasks are completed during this time and you are feeling "good" about getting things done, it is **NOT** the task that needs time, effort and focus. Typically this type of procrastination is used when the task requires lots of time and energy **OR** when there is a distinct aversion to accomplishing the task.

Generally, the "fear trigger" kicks up the *"ill wind of procrastination."* Whether it is fear of not doing the task well, not knowing how to do the task but afraid to ask, not wanting to experience reprisal if the task is NOT completed, or fear of success (as in downsizing and turning a new chapter in my life), it is fear nonetheless. And, the fallout or the aftermath of procrastination stemming from fear can cause rejection, shame, anxiety, blame, relationship problems, financial loss and a misplaced character perception such as being lazy, uncaring and untrustworthy.

So, the next time you feel the "ill wind of procrastination" swirling around you, take these steps:

1. Apply a little B.A.L.M. to support your effort in breaking a negative pattern and claiming self-improvement. **B.A.L.M.** stands for **believe, accept, love, me**.

2. Learn to say NO. Govern your time accordingly or you will always sacrifice your best.

3. Create a "lifeline" before it is needed which is designed to salvage not demean your spirit e.g. mini-mental vacation; bartering the task; delegate the task and attack the task in bite size increments.

4. Seek the assistance of a life coach to support your transformation in breaking a negative pattern and claiming self-improvement.

Procrastination is in our DNA so expect it to *"puff up"* at times. As in the manner in which it *blew through my home* when I needed to downsize, it can also pay you a visit. But don't despair because there are ways to *"quell its ill wind"*. First, recognize what it is and how you feel about it. Second, listen to your inner dialogue, bringing clarity in defining **WHY** it *"swirls around your head"* and **HOW** to deflate its power. Last, **MAKE A MENTAL NOTE** of what you did to turn the *"wind into a breeze"* and shift its direction so that it *exits your home*. Once you build your self-improvement guide and put it into action, you, too, can claim your expiration date!

My Favorites

Scripture
My help comes from the Lord, the Maker of heaven and earth. He will not let your foot slip --- he who watches over you will not slumber: Psalm 121: 2-3 NIV

Favorite Quote

"The two most important days in your life are the day you are born and the day you find out why!" ~ Mark Twain

Personal Quote

"Endeavor to reach the 'Zenith' in you." ~

Coacheyemore

Poem

"After a While"
~ By Veronica A. Shoffstall

~ Coach Iris T. Moore

I have always found that my signature coaching tool is self-discovery through self-analysis. The following books have been abundantly helpful in supporting that journey.... ~ **CoachEYEMORE**

Illustrations by Coacheyemore

Want your *F.E.A.R.* (False expectations altering reality) to have an expiration date? Face it!

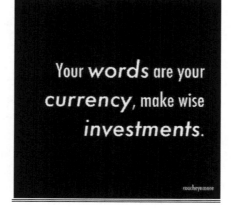

Quotes by Coacheyemore

Testimonials

Several years ago I was given a book entitled <u>Strengths Finder</u>. The author asks, "Do you have the opportunity to do what you do best every day?" For the past twenty years I have had the opportunity to work with, report to, and become friends with Iris Moore. Iris clearly has lived what she does best every day as a leader, mentor and life coach. When she was my manager, I could count on Iris' realistic and challenging situational analysis as well as constructive feedback, which resulted most often in success. I was given <u>Strengths Finder</u> by Iris. This valuable tool helped me to uncover strategies and enhance my talents.

Leslie Y. Baker, Tallahassee, FL

CoachEyeMore's Life Coaching enhanced my L.I.F.E by making me more Logical, Insightful, Fulfilled, and Enlightened. I have become more Logical by systematically addressing problems to make resolution more manageable. I have become Insightful to life themes that consistently present in various situations. I have become more Fulfilled because I better understand situations that are leading me towards my calling in life. Lastly, I am more Enlightened regarding life. I have an optimism that has come alive from the conversations and exercises that bring together fragmented life pieces to make my picture of purpose more clear and focused.

Tyrone McCloud, Physician Liaison. Jacksonville, FL

From left, me, my Mom (Ernestine), Harold Jr., William and sweet little Kevin on a chilly Easter morning. Long Island 1964.

*As you walk through your seasons of life, be comforted that self-actualization often is the very vehicle that sometimes drops you off at unfamiliar destinations. At that moment, that very moment, you are most open to learning something new! So, take a deep breath and a step forward to embrace that feeling because your investment will be so worthwhile your effort. ~ **Coacheyemore***

Contact Coach Iris T. Moore

Coach Iris T. Moore
Business Name: Coacheyemore
Business Line: (904) 651-4344
Website: www.coacheyemore.com
Email: transform@coacheyemore.com

Frequently Asked Questions (FAQ)

1. ***Why would anyone need or desire to be coached?*** Sometimes we need a little help; a little encouragement; a little cheering; and some accountability in order to make changes and quality decisions in our lives. Coaching could prove to be the missing link.

2. ***What constitutes a "good Life Coach?"*** For starters, a good Life Coach is one who has invested in himself/herself by completing a structured training process, thereby becoming certified to offer Life Coaching services. A good Life Coach must have a genuine love for people and a strong desire to see people win at life. A good Life Coach must be a good listener. Because we are all unique, it is imperative to select a good Life Coach which will be the "best fit" for the individual seeking services. No one Life Coach is the "best fit" for everyone.

3. ***How do I go about finding a good Life Coach?*** The Life Coaches featured within this book would be a great starting point. Contact information for each Life Coach is listed at the end of each Coach's chapter, as well as in the directory at the end of this book. Other means of selecting a good Life Coach would include: personal research and referrals. Stop and think. I'm sure you can come up with additional options.

4. ***How do you find your Clients?*** My number one means of securing new Clients is by referrals. Investing in maintaining updated social media sites such as LinkedIn and Face Book have produced numerous new Clients. Public appearances, advertisements, and current marketing materials can also lead to new Clients. Consistency and commitment to the vocation are very important factors. Having a "ready to deliver" elevator speech proves competency and could lead to new Clients. Having business cards readily available and wearing my business name badge are instrumental also.

5. ***How often does a Client meet with the Life Coach?*** The frequency is contingent upon the agreement made between the Coach and the Client. How often would you like to meet?

6. ***How much does it cost to hire a Life Coach?*** Do your research. Prices vary. Keep in mind, "you get what you pay for." In other words, don't let pricing be the deciding factor in selecting a Coach.

~ Coach J Dianne Tribble

The Little Engine that Could talked himself into destiny and set an exemplary example. He kept saying and believing, "I think I can! I think I can..." And as we know, he did! You can too.

~ Coach J Dianne Tribble

~ Life Story Three ~
Coach Gigi Blackshear

Author and Certified Christian Life Coach Gigi Blackshear is a native of Jacksonville, Florida. An avid reader, writer, motivational speaker and inspirational Life Coach, Gigi received her Life Coach training and certification through At the Table Life Coaching and Motivational Speaking Services LLC. As founder of Conscious Choice Coaching, Gigi thoroughly enjoys empowering and equipping others to see their true value and worth according to the word of God. Her coaching practice teaches that we can all create the lives we desire, one choice at a time.

A lifelong writer and journaler, Gigi realized her dream of becoming an Author with the release of her first book, <u>Thank You for the Pain: Poems and Reflections on the Journey to Gratitude</u> in 2011 and has been a featured Author in Entrepreneur's Anchor, Guidepost and Ezine Articles. Gifted as an encourager, Gigi uses her writing to uplift the spirits of friends, family members, and strangers alike.

Gigi is employed by JM Family Enterprises as Marketing Manager for JM Associates Federal Credit Union. A dedicated member of Spirit of Life Worship Center, Gigi serves as Sunday school teacher and Steward Board member.

The mother of two wonderful adult sons and grandmother of three beautiful grandkids, Gigi loves to travel and enjoys spending time with her family and beloved dog Duncan.

Answering My Heart's Cry

Coach Gigi Blackshear

Have you ever had a feeling so strong that it would not let you sleep at night? A feeling that you could not shake no matter what you did? Well, that feeling was the driving force behind my decision to become a Life Coach. You see, I had spent my whole life giving advice. I had always been told that it was because I was a great listener. Family members and friends alike sought me out for answers to all kinds of dilemmas.

There had also been a constant stream of circumstances and situations that brought complete strangers into my life in which I was able to help, just by listening and giving counsel. I knew that the ability to help others find answers and solve their problems was a gift, because it always seemed to be the right answer, the perfect solution, and it always worked! I did not quite understand what this was, this ability, but somehow I was able to listen between the words to hear the heart of the person speaking, and that was where their answers were to be found. God allowed me to listen intently enough to hear them. I knew that God had a plan and a purpose for this gift. My heart's desire was to find out what that purpose was.

Because I believe that (when we allow Him to) God orchestrates our lives, I spent many months in prayer. I sought the Lord and my prayer was this "Lord, if this is what you have for me, show me what it is and what you want me to do with it." The Bible says that faith without works is dead, so while I waited, I began talking to people and searching online, trying to find out as much as I possibly could.

That is where I discovered Life Coaching as a career. I discovered that there were many schools and training courses designed to "teach" you how to become a Life Coach. There were also as many coaches advertising to "coach" coaches as there were schools. For a while, I contacted different schools and tried to compare programs and packages, but quickly became quite overwhelmed by the whole process. There were so many and they all varied so much in what they offered and in what they charged for their programs.

It quickly became obvious to me that this "life coach" thing was the new popular "thing." I discovered that Life Coaching as a profession was a relatively new field and still yet unregulated. I also discovered that many of those calling themselves "Life Coaches" had not had any formal training at all. This was, in my opinion, at the very least, reckless. Because I wanted to know more, I continued to pray and wait.

God led me, through an acquaintance, to an organization called the First Coast Coaches Association (FCCA). This group is the local chapter of the International Coaching Federation (ICF). My friend suggested that I contact the FCCA as a resource for information. Within this organization, I found others like myself that had felt an initial gifting in this area and had followed their dreams to become Certified Life Coaches.

After attending a couple of meetings, I actually joined the FCCA. I wanted to learn as much as possible about Life Coaching from people that were actually doing what believed I was called to do. Upon spending time with real coaches, I decided that I definitely wanted to become a Life Coach. I began my search in earnest for a training program that would provide me with the necessary training and credentials to become a Certified Life Coach.

Seek and Ye Shall Find

While on the internet one afternoon, I ran across an article entitled *You Can't Live Yesterday Today: Maximizing Performance and Expectations In Your New Role*, by J. Dianne Tribble, Life Coach and Motivational Speaker. After reading the article, I was intrigued. Here was a woman that looked like me and according to the article, sounded like me, and was doing the exact thing that I believed that God had called me to. I had to meet her. I visited Ms. Tribble's website and contacted her in reference to her complimentary 30 minute coaching session. Even though I had no interest in being coached, I wanted to pick her brain about coaching as a profession. Little did I know, this meeting would be a pivotal turning point in my life. God had led me to the exact person I needed to help me move forward in my quest to become a Life Coach.

Ms. Tribble and I agreed to meet at a local restaurant for lunch and I was instantly impressed with her mannerisms and her straight forward approach. I knew immediately that this lady was a professional and that she was serious about what she was doing -not just some fly-by-night that had hung up a card board sign calling herself a "Life Coach." Unfortunately, I had met many of those.

What I enjoyed most about meeting her was that there was no "hard sell." As a matter of fact, she allowed me to do the most of the talking. Even though initially I had no desire to be coached, unbeknownst to me, I had placed myself into the hands of a master coach. At the end of our meeting, I knew two things, first, that this encounter had been God ordained and secondly, He truly does make provision for what He orders. I left confident that I had found my calling and was ready to move forward.

More than Notion A

During my rigorous training process there were many days when my flesh wanted to back out of the training, especially after a long day at work, with chapters to read still yet ahead of me. But what kept me going was the support of my trainer and the unquenchable desire to see this through. During the process, as I prayed that God would help me learn as much as I could. He ministered to me that someone was waiting for this particular gift to be fully matured. There were also days when my flesh asked me "Do you really need to be trained to do what you have been doing your whole life anyway?" I learned early on not to listen to my flesh.

What I discovered during training, and why I believe formal training is so vitally important, is that people are hurting. The answers they seek require so much more than a kind word of encouragement or a hug. Granted, I have given out more than my share of those, but hurting people need real solutions to real problems and coaching is one way to help them. While Life Coaching may be the "new thing," Life Coaching as a profession is more than a notion and definitely not for the timid or faint at heart. As a matter of fact, for me it was much more than a notion, it was and still is a mission. Is your heart crying out to you? Perhaps it is time to answer.

Unwrapped and Unafraid

They say confession is good for the soul and James 5:16 says "confess your faults one to another and pray for one another that you may be healed, The effective, fervent prayers of the righteous availeth much."

Today, I confess that I was afraid! Not afraid of you, not afraid of standing before you, because as my fellow coaches I believe that we all have felt fear at one time or another. Not even afraid of failure, but afraid of being successful.

You see, God had given me a gift, a beautifully wrapped package of talents. You have all probably heard me say, or read my business card which says, God is the giver of gifts and talents, how are you using yours? That is my mantra.

Yes, God had given me a gift which I received with great joy. I recognized the value of the gift and had every intention of using it until fear stepped in. You see, up until I received the gift, I was busy being "Gigi" and I am good at that! That's my comfortable place, No fear there!

Along with my gift, God even gave me the perfect analogy, you may have heard it, "It's like the doors in front of the grocery store, you can stand across the street and you can yell at the doors, you can pray at them, you can even shabach them, but those doors will only open when you walk towards them"

Well, I held my gift in my hand and I even walked towards those doors and guess what? True to my analogy, they opened right up! As soon as I took a step to go through those doors fear spoke to me. Fear said, "Now that you have the gift, you have to be somebody else. Gigi is not good enough!" fear said, "You're not ready, you don't have enough education. You don't know anything about running a business, not yet, maybe later. Go back to school. Go get some more training. You're just not good enough!" And I listened.

Because I was afraid, I did not walk through those doors. I stood in front of them paralyzed by fear. At times, I paced back and forth because I knew, in my heart that I was supposed to be on the other side of those doors, but I was afraid.

As I stood there, I pondered and I prayed! I told God, I know you gave me this gift. Why am I afraid? He answered by saying, "You are afraid because, although you received the gift, you never opened it!" Imagine that! I had received the gift, I was grateful for it, excited about it, but before I even had the opportunity to open it, fear spoke to me and had succeeded in preventing me from opening the gift God had given me.

Has fear spoken to anyone else in here or am I the only one? I looked at the still wrapped gift in my hands and I looked at the opened doors, and yes, they were still opened. I believe grace and mercy held the doors opened for me. You see, as I stood there, others were going through those doors, getting their blessings and having their dreams fulfilled.

I nervously unwrapped the gift God had given me, and to my surprise, inside the beautifully wrapped package was ME! God said,

"You don't have the gift, you are the gift exactly as I created you to be."

Today I stand before you unwrapped and Unafraid! I am the gift!

~ Coach Gigi Blackshear

Using My Christian Life Coach Certification

Today, I am using my Life Coach certification in my business, Conscious Choice Coaching. Initially, after receiving my certification, I was ready to take on the world. God had already given me the name for my business. I created a website and ordered business cards. I was ready, or so I thought. I made the rounds of "coaching" events, I networked with other coaches. I had even already joined a professional coaching organization. However, what I discovered was that not only was Life Coaching as a profession more than a notion, so was running a business.

I was faced with the stark reality that I knew absolutely nothing about running a successful business. And I immediately became filled with fear. Although I was afraid of what I did not know, I also knew that there is no reason to "not know" anything in this day and age. I knew that I did not need to recreate the wheel. All I needed to do is exactly what I had done to become a Coach, find the resources that were available and learn what I needed to know to operate my own business.

Today I am actively coaching clients and am looking forward to seeing my business grow. Not everyone that receives Life Coach training and certification is doing it for the purpose of going into business. Once you have acquired the training and knowledge to successfully coach someone, you can use these skills in every part of your life. Keeping in mind, if you have been called to this, your gift will make room for you and bring you before great men.

What Life Coaching is Not

Life Coaching is not counseling or psycho-analyzing,

Life Coaching is not a confessional or anger management treatment,

Life Coaching is not a therapy session or a treatment for medical malaise.

What Life Coaching Is

Life Coaching is an alliance between the coach and the Client fostered by a mutual agreement of trust and accountability. Within this structure, the Client develops the necessary skills to address specific issues in their life. Using the Coaching methodology as a support structure for change, overtime, the Client will gain clarity, confidence and the ability to make positive, conscious choices that will create an effective, balanced and fulfilling life.

~ Coach Gigi Blackshear

Letting Go, the Exercise!

By Coach Gigi Blackshear

Sometimes the things that limit our progress, our ability to move forward are not the things that are in front of us, such as lack of education or opportunity. Sometimes the things that are hindering us are the things behind us. Old relationships, commitments and even memories can keep us stuck in the past. This exercise is designed to bring clarity and allow the client to realize the freedom of being able to walk away from the ties of the past to a brighter, happier future.

Tools needed:

Assorted sized bungee cords, fixed or weighted stationary object.

 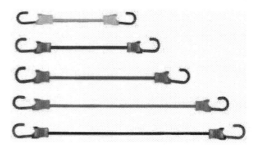

During the conversation, the client share the reason(s) he/she believes he/she cannot move forward. For every reason given, the client is handed a bungee that he/she selects. The size of the bungee is based on the client's belief as to the complexity or difficulty of the limiting issue. One hooked ends of the bungee(s) is attached to an immovable, fixed object. (I use my desk).

After attaching the bungee(s) to the immovable object, the Client is handed the opposite end of the bungee and instructed to move forward. Client attempts to walk away with bungee in hand. Realizing that he/she can only move so far away, the Client complains about the bungee. The Coach ask client to explain why he/she cannot move forward. The light bulb comes on! The client recognizes that the reason he/she can't move forward is because he/she is holding onto the bungee. The bungee is not holding on to him/her.

Some Clients will attempt to keep moving forward by attempting to drag the desk behind them. When posed questions pertaining to pay off or possible benefit of dragging the heavy weight, the light bulb comes on. As clients address each bungee of life, usually the smaller ones first, they let go.

This exercise can be used in groups, as well as in individual coaching sessions. It is especially powerful in group settings when Clients assist each other with the letting go process.

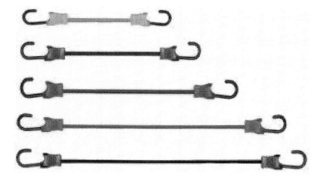

My Favorites

Scripture

"For I know the thoughts that I think toward you, saith the LORD, thoughts of peace, and not of evil, to give you an expected end." ~ Jeremiah 29:11

Quote

"Our lives are the sum total of our choices" ~ Wayne Dyer

Personal Quote

"God is the giver of gifts and talents, how are you using yours?" ~ Coach Gigi Blackshear

Poem

"Still I Rise" ~ Maya Angelou

~ Coach Gigi Blackshear

Top Recommended Reading List

1. Thank You For The Pain: Poems and Reflections on the Journey to Gratitude by Coach Gigi Blackshear (2011)
2. The Power of Eve: It's Not What You Think by Coach Gigi Blackshear (2014)
3. The Alchemist by Paulo Coelho (2009)
4. Three Feet From Gold by Sharon L. Lechter & Greg Reid (2009)
5. The War of Art by Steven Pressfield & Shawn Coyne (2002)

Coach Gigi Blackshear's Contact Information:
Conscious Choice Coaching
Gigi Blackshear
gerovani@msn.com
(904)239-2320
www.gigiblackshear.com
www.facebook.com/gblackshear
Twitter.com @gerovani

Testimonial

A Coach for Life

I truly believe God brings people in your life for a reason and those that are standing by you when you're going through your storm and there to see you through until the end are the ones that he meant to be there and I must say he has truly blessed my life with some awesome sister friends. Oct 2005 when I started at JM Family he blessed my life with another awesome woman. Gigi, I'm still trying to figure out why you'd always put me out your office and call me Miss Daisy.

I did not know at the time the reason God brought you into my life, but in Jan 2010, I then understood why. I have many friends, but Jan. 2010 I lost my BFF, I would talk to her maybe 6 times a day, sometimes more. She was the angel of my life, my "Mother", and none of my girlfriends had experienced such a lost at the time,

I also did not know Gigi that you had lost your mother to the same disease that took mine, Cancer, so you understood when a daughter is so close to her mother and the loss I'd feel. I also did not know at the time that before my mother's passing that you all had a conversation about me.

I know my mother needed me to continue to be the strong woman she raised me to be, but the loss of her may be truly hard test for me. Gigi you assured her that you would watch over me kind of like my Guardian Angel and you've been there every since encouraging me, lifting me up when I felt I could not go on. I prayed that God would bless my life with a church home and through you and one visit to Spirit of Life, I knew I was home.

You prayed for me & my boys even when I didn't know you were, My son Austin has adopted you as his second mother and will come to you sometimes and not me on things in his life when he needs encouraging or prayed for . Whenever the devil is attacking me and my family, two things I always remember are your words "God's got you, Miss Daisy & there is nothing too hard for God".

I thank God for you my sister and being there for me all the times I felt like my life was in shambles. Sometimes people look at you from the outside and think you have it all together not knowing your going through a storm on the inside. Thank you Gigi for your encouragement, prayers and for honoring my mother wishes by just being there for me.

I don't know if this is a testimony to your skills as a life coach because I had no idea I was being coached. I only know that with every question you asked me, I was made better. You have used your gift to be a blessing to me and my family. I am forever grateful. If this is coaching, you will be my coach for life.

Love You,
Miss Daisy (Phelanda)

~ *Coach Gigi Blackshear*

Build Yourself Up!

My Clients are required to have four tools readily available during each Coaching session. These four tools are: **paper, pen, a Bible, and a mirror.** Capturing their own notes and action steps are the responsibility of the Client. Writing these things down are not only beneficial in assisting the Clients to remember, but they also serve as excellent accountability tools. By writing "it" down, the likelihood of goals being completed by Clients greatly increase.

As a Christian Life Coach, the Bible is used as an essential reference in encouraging my Clients in the areas in which they elect to work on. While the Bible may not be used during every session, having it readily available helps in maximizing the Clients' sessions without interrupted time as they run to retrieve their Bibles.

The mirror is a powerful coaching tool. While I do my part in actively affirming my Clients, it is just as important (if not more so) for the Clients to affirm themselves. Looking into the mirror, I might ask one of the following questions:

1. What do you see?
2. Who are you?
3. Take a step of faith and affirm yourself while looking in the mirror.
4. What does God have to say about you?
5. What do you like about yourself?
6. What do you know needs to change in your life?
7. Please complete this sentence, "To be honest, I _____."

This has proven to be a transforming exercise time after time. One of my loyal Clients shared with me the great effect this exercise had on her. When she was asked to look in the mirror and respond to the question, "Who are you," she cried and cried because she did not know who she was at that time. However, since that time, she has gone on to do big and exciting things.

While working with another Client, the mirror exercise was used to build her self-esteem up to a healthy status. She grew so comfortable with the mirror that she began to make self-affirming declarations about herself. We took it a step further by having her build a Declaration Board. Confidently, she shared her Declaration Board during one of my workshops. Knowing how much it had helped her, she was willing to share the board and the impact it had upon her life with others.

Over the years, I have found that the mirror exercise is instrumental in initiating the healing process. We are what we say. Proverbs 18:21 states: "Death and life are in the **power** of the tongue: and they that love it shall eat the fruit thereof." The mirror exercise definitely builds my Clients up. Give it a try.

What are you challenged to do as a result of reading "Build Yourself Up?"

_____
_____
_____

~ Coach J Dianne Tribble

~ *Life Story Four* ~

Coach Shara Mondy

Shara Mondy *is a successful non-profit expert consultant, corporate speaker and Certified Professional Concierge Lifestyle Coach specializing in "Business Beauty Bling". She is one of the most respected and sought-after advocates on transitional and supportive services for men and women, and professional image in the workplace. She is the CEO and Founder of a successful and nationally recognized non-profit organization,* **Suited For Success** ™ *which provides interview attire and job readiness assistance to clients who are in transition, seeking employment. Mondy has been providing these services for over 10 years and is still going strong* *with support from Celebrity Spokesperson, Actor/Author/Motivational Speaker, Tommy Ford and corporate partner, The Men's Wearhouse, which supports Mondy's organization with clothing during the Men's Wearhouse National Suit Drive. The Suit Drive takes place annually and Suited For Success has been the Charity to benefit from the suit drive for the past seven years. To learn more visit my website at www.suited4success.com.*

Mondy has been providing Coaching services for the past 20 years focusing on career coaching and personal and professional development. After having so many requests from newly referred clients wanting more one-on-one coaching in all areas of their lives, especially how to develop their business and passions, she decided to expand her Coaching services by becoming certified as a Christian Lifestyle Coach. Having spent over 25 years as a Licensed Cosmetologist and Salon Owner and 10 years working as a Celebrity Personal Assistant, Mondy knows a thing or two about inspiring others to achieve their personal and professional goals. Coaching is the tool Mondy is using to help her clients turn their "Passions into Profits".

Mondy is a frequent media guest featured in the Florida Times Union Newspaper, local publications and Motivational Speaker in Jacksonville, Florida, and has been interviewed on every network in her local area with the most recent story spotlight on July 15, 2014 (News4Jax) in a feature story promoting the Men's Wearhouse National Suit drive. Suited For Success has also gained headlines on the national circuit in The Ladies Home Journal Magazine with a Headline of "Never Underestimate the Power of A Woman" and the article entitled "Well Suited" in the June 2010 issue. She has been noted as being a successful non-profit expert, motivational speaker and advocate.

Why I became a Certified Life Coach

My "WHY" became a reality to me when I realized that I was already providing Coaching services to people who wanted to meet with me to talk about helping them start or grow their business. I was getting referrals from so many different people who I helped at one point in their early stages of sorting out the details of what they wanted to do either for personal goals or business goals. Your time is valuable, and your God given talents are even more valuable.

I learned a valuable lesson from my mentor and friend, "People will not respect your Business as a Business, until you run your Business like a Business."

How I'm using My Certification Today

I have been working for over 10 years as a Celebrity Personal Assistant and I am still working with some very high profile Celebrities, Actors and Athletes who have partnered with me, as well as providing me some great opportunities to participate in Motivational tours, Expos, Panel Discussions. Now I am expanding my Coaching to include my own Coaching Brand called "Business Beauty Bling" (B3), which is a Boutique Business Coaching and Consulting Group. We help our clients get to the next level and turn their Passions into Profits.

This unique coaching program was designed for clients to experience the ultimate business mentoring opportunity to help them create the successful life and business of their dreams!

~ Coach Shara Mondy

SIMPLY SHARA.... PURPOSE, PASSION PROFITS

Learning to walk into your Purpose with Passion and Profit during the process.

So you want to be a Life Coach?

Let me share with you why I decided to become a Life Coach.

My story simply begins with having the heart of a servant. I enjoy helping people become better people in all areas of their lives. I began my journey in Coaching over 10 years ago when the term Coaching was not as commonly used or as it is now known to be looked at as a career term for helping people achieve their personal, professional, spiritual, financial, emotional and passionate goals. Let me spend a little more time breaking down this Coaching thing. Let's start with the question behind this book project. **"So You Want to Be a Coach?"** Let's see if your reasons are similar to my personal reasons for taking my Coaching career to the next level.

C. is for **"CHRIST"**- My Counselor, Confidant and Coach. When I decided to go forward and pursue this Coaching thing that I heard so much about, the first step I took was talking with my Coach in all areas of my life, **"CHRIST."**

***O*. is for "OBEDIENT"-** You have to know that God is talking to you, supporting you, pushing you, and motivating you to move forward in your purpose. Once that is understood, you must then be **"OBEDIENT"** to the journey.

***A*. is for "ACTION"-** Simply put, "Faith without works is dead." Once you consult Christ, be Obedient to His Word, then you must apply the **"ACTION"** to bring your dream to reality.

***C*. is for "COURAGE"-** One of my favorite sayings lately seems to be, "When life throws you Lemons, Make Lemonade." Trust me, once you set your mind on Success, get ready for some Lemons. That's where the **"COURAGE"** comes into play. You have to be bold and press through to the end.

***H*. is for "HAPPY"-** At the end of the day, you must be happy with your life choices and learn to accept the things that you cannot change, learn from them, and change the things that you can change. We don't always make the right choices, but thank God for allowing grace to enter our life to help us to find our **"HAPPY"** and learn to LIVE, LOVE, LAUGH AND LEARN.

That is why I decided to become a Coach and use my life lessons to guide in my Coaching process which leads to another very important level of making life choices when it comes to your personal and professional life.

There comes a time in your life when I feel everyone should perform a "Life Audit." Well, you ask, "What is a Life Audit?" My personal definition of a "Life Audit" is when you consciously sit down and take a self-evaluation of your life. I did this for myself when I was trying to decide if I was going to pursue my passion full time or just do it as a ministry. I created a checklist that eventually grew more intense as I was reviewing some life decisions and life challenges. So, I decided to create a system that would simplify this process and also give me a format that would keep me on track with reaching my goals. That is how my Five "W" Life Audit™ system was designed and now I use this same system in my Lifestyle Coaching Business.

Let's talk about a "Life Audit"....

On the road to "Excellence," there will always be obstacles, but it's the way you handle the obstacles that will determine your success. Just start by asking yourself some key questions which will help lay the foundation for you to build your business. There are many layers to starting a business and having your life in check will be the fuel that will jump start your walk into your *PURPOSE*, give you the *PASSION* and help create the *PROFIT* that will make you a success in your goals.

As a Certified Lifestyle Coach, I have built my business by starting with a few key "Steps to Success" and I have tried to stay true to these steps throughout my career. First and foremost, Plan your business around your *"PASSION"*. When you are doing something you love doing, you will give it 100% at all times. Your *PASSION* will shine through to your current and potential customers. People feed off of your energy.

Secondly, Begin with a Plan. As they say, "Plan your work and work your plan." You have to complete your "Life Audit" so that you will be clear about what your goals are and what is driving you. Once you know your true direction, your *"PASSION"* will overflow into your *"PURPOSE"* and the *"PROFITS"* will start to flow.

Lastly, create your own "Daily Pledge", "Daily Mantra" or "Daily Meditation Moments" which will help keep you on track and focused on reaching your desired dreams and goals.

In the pursuit of *"PURPOSE"*, here are some things that I want you to pay close attention to and make sure that you have performed your "Life Audit" before trying to figure out if you are in line with your *"PURPOSE"*. The first thing that you must do is check your surroundings. Ask yourself some key questions that will immediately show you that you are or are not on the path to *PURPOSE*. If things in the Good column outweigh the Bad column, then you may be on your way.

One thing that I did personally during my "Life Audit" was to shift my mindset. Have you ever heard the saying, "Surround yourself with the positive people that you would like to become?" For example, I did not have a mentor or Coach when I started my journey to becoming an entrepreneur. Therefore, I made some costly mistakes because I did not have a role model to follow or a template to work from that outlined the positives and the negatives of doing business as an entrepreneur.

I grew up like most people early on in their business career, I had a 9 to 5 J.O.B (Just Over Broke) that I relied on to support me and my family. It did not take me into the area of financing my desire to be self-employed. There was always more month than money.

So, I started researching successful people that I had admired as I was growing up. I started following their work habits, social habits and financial habits. I started reading books on being successful which were written by people just like me who started out with nothing, but the *PASSION* inside them fueled their desire to press onward and upward pursuing their *PURPOSE*. I also connected with a mentor who was doing what I wanted to do. She helped me map out my path to success without all of the pitfalls that you can encounter when you don't have a plan.

When it comes to *PASSION,* which is something that I truly believe that God instills in each and every one of us and it is up to us to nurture and grow our *PASSION* to become the driving force behind our PURPOSE. Another tool that I use in my Coaching business, is to pick your top three areas of *PASSION* and then describe how each area makes you feel when you are doing something that you truly love. This exercise can really help polish your plan towards turning your *PASSION* into *PROFIT.*

Last but definitely not least, let's talk about that wonderful word "*PROFIT*". Not only does it provide the financial security to continue to support our business and personal goals, it allows you to be able to enjoy the fruits of your labor. That's why the specialty of my Coaching business as a "Certified Lifestyle Coach" allows me to focus on all areas of a person's life, while enjoying my *PASSION* areas of Business, Beauty, and Bling.

I center my Coaching services around the things I really enjoy doing and use them to help Clients to develop those areas within their own personal and professional lives. I have been a Career Coach and Celebrity Personal Assistant for over 10 years, a Cosmetologist and former salon owner for over 20 years, and started my own jewelry business, featuring bold statement pieces from my "Bling Queen" Collection. I strive to live my life on *PURPOSE* with *PASSION* and make a *PROFIT.*

My Daily Mantra: Live Life to the Fullest Daily, and Live it "BY DESIGN, NOT BY DEFAULT"

If you would like to register for one of my Business Beauty Bling Boot camps or One-on-One Lifestyle Coaching sessions, please send me an email at: **businessbeautybling@gmail.com** and I will be sure to contact you with more information. I look forward to sharing in your journey to *PURPOSE PASSION PROFIT.*

Simply Shara

"Be happy (in your faith) and rejoice and be glad, hearted continually". ~ I Thessalonians 5:16 (AMP)

FIVE "W" LIFE AUDIT SYSTEM™
Created by: Shara Mondy, Certified Lifestyle Coach

WHO

Who Am I? This is where you can confidently, without a self-doubt, boldly look yourself in the mirror and say 'Who Am I?' You can determine who you are by giving your one minute elevator speech or with your personal affirmation. (Hint) If you do not have either a one minute elevator speech or a personal affirmation, then you really have work to do and I am available to assist you in a Lifestyle Coaching capacity to help you develop your personal Five "W" Life Audit.™

WHAT

What is my Purpose? This area is a little more intense and will require some prayer and meditation with God to make sure that you are walking in the purpose that God has designed for your life. This process comes sooner for some than others. It is definitely a personal journey that has to be reached through a personal connection with Wisdom, Strength and Understanding.

WHEN

When? NOW. This is a short and simple answer, especially if you don't have the "WHO" or "WHAT" answered. You have to learn to live in the "NOW", slow down and savor the moment called "NOW." Life is too short. All we have is the right now moments to be prepared in the event that God allows you to wake up tomorrow and be a part of the "TODAY" that a new day brings.

WHERE

Where do I start? Here is a good place to start, I will share my daily "Mantra" that I use to keep me on track with my personal life goals and keeps me on track to living my "Purpose."

I strive to constantly renew myself daily by focusing on the four dimensions of my life:
BODY, SPIRIT, MIND, SOUL

- BODY: Treat my body as the Temple that God intended it to be
- SPIRIT: Continue to practice self-love, continue to meditate daily and seek God's face and continue to show God's love to all
- MIND: Continue to seek knowledge and education in the areas that will grow my business and increase my financial growth.
- SOUL: Surround myself with positive people who are mentally, physically, spiritually and financially headed in the same direction that I am pursuing.

WHY

Why? This is a great question and the best way that I can describe the reason this is a key element of the Life Audit is with one word, "DEATH." I know some of you gasp, and think, "Why in the world would she use that word?" Thanks for asking. I will tell you "WHY."

Death forces us to look at "LIFE". It boldly reminds us to re-evaluate our own lives and how we are living. The advice I would give in this area is with an exercise that I use in my Coaching business and that is to have my clients to write their own Eulogy. Yes, I said Eulogy.

Well, I have shared some valuable key tips and tools that I use in my Lifestyle Coaching business. They have become great training tools in my workshops, conferences, and business boot camps.

Testimonials

Darrell Grooms, Consultant, RSE Consulting: I started volunteering for Coach Shara's non-profit organization, Suited for Success over 8 years ago and she began mentoring me on the process of running a successful non-profit organization. I was in the process of just starting out in the corporate arena and I was attracted to the idea of being an entrepreneur. So, Coach Shara sat down with me for a discovery session on what I wanted to focus on and from there I became a client and she really helped me to set some basic foundation goals and develop my own progress report to help me stay focused on my end result. I am still working with her two years, later after I developed and redesigned my full business plan for expanding my consulting firm. I really enjoyed using her Five "W" Life Audit system. It really made me sit down and focus on some key life and business goals.

Ronline Canady, Certified Christian Life Coach: Coach Shara and I have been friends for over 10 years. I have had the opportunity to be a part of some of her events, and witnessed her in action with some of her clients and celebrity business partners, such as Tommy Ford. I enjoyed seeing how she used very basic steps to get her clients thinking about their goals and then hearing so many success stories about their progress. It made me revisit some of my own personal goals of doing more with the clients that I counseled in ministry. I took the next step in taking my passion to the next level and now I am proud to say that I too am a Certified Christian Life Coach. Thanks Coach Shara for your mentoring, support and encouragement.

My Favorites

Scripture

"Trust in the Lord with all your heart, And lean not on your own understanding".

Proverbs 3:5 (NKJV)

Quote

"Failure is not the opposite of Success, It's the stepping stone to Success."
~ Arianna Huffington's mother

Personal Quote

"I live life on Purpose, Not by default."

~ Coach Shara Mondy

Poem

"My Purpose Gave Birth to Me"

~ By: Iyanla Vanzant

~ Coach Shara Mondy

Top Recommended Reading List

1. The Bible
2. When God Speaks to my Heart: A Daybook of Personal Moments with God (2005) by Rosalie Willis
3. Eat, Pray, Love (2007) by Elizabeth Gilbert
4. Act Like a Success, Think like a Success (2014) by Steve Harvey
5. Instinct (2014) by Bishop T.D. Jakes.

Coach Shara Mondy, CPCLC

Certified Professional Concierge Life Coach, specializing in

Business Beauty Bling

Mobile: (904) 333-3555

Email: sharamondy@gmail.com

Email: businessbeautybling@gmail.com

www.businessbeautybling.com

Facebook:www.facebook.com/shara.mondy

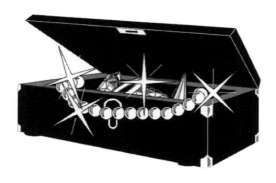

I invite you to visit my non-profit organizations website, Suited For Success Jacksonville, Inc., and learn more about my community service and outreach program that was featured in the June 2010 issue of the Ladies Home Journal Magazine.

www.suited4success.com

Simply Shara

Picture Gallery

Coach J Dianne Tribble

C.O.A.C.H. CHARACTER ACRONYM

C – CONFIDANT

O – OPTIMISTIC

A – ATTENTIVE

C – CHEERFUL

H – HELPFUL

The character of a Life Coach is marked by the following characteristics: confident confidant, optimistic, attentive, cheerful, and helpful. Our Clients can safely confide in us and draw strength from the confidence we walk in. Our optimism is used as a beacon to keep our Clients energized and motivated to keep moving forward. Because we are attentive, it assures our Clients that we really do have their best interest at heart. Exhibiting a cheerful countenance serves as a great dose of encouragement and affirmation. Helping our Clients to succeed is at the heart of all we do.   I♥ Life Coaching! ~ *Coach J Dianne Tribble*

Life brings experience. Experience qualifies you to help others. Whether your experiences have been good or bad, there will be times when people are strategically placed in your path, desperately in need of what you possess (experience). Resist being the best kept secret when your secret can be instrumental in helping others. Keep moving forward.   ~ Coach J Dianne Tribble

~ Life Story Five ~

Coach Alvin W. King

I am a Certified Professional Life Coach/Trainer, Financial Coach, and a Motivational Speaker. My picture of passion is to assist others with living life without limits; achieve financial freedom; and inspire them to reach their destinies in life. As a Life Coach, I become the "change agent" in supporting and encouraging others to bring out their best and taking the plunge to reach their destinies.

As a Financial Coach, my desire is to educate individuals on how to establish and achieve realistic financial goals which will reward them with the financial freedom to live out their dreams and "pay it forward" while enjoying life.

As a Motivational Speaker, I encourage individuals in the community with living out their purposes in life. I am available to meet in one-on-one sessions, group sessions, organizations, churches, and other settings, in providing Infinite Solutions around the world.

Professional Life Coach Credentials:
Life Coach and Life Coach Trainer certification from At the Table
Life Coaching & Motivational Speaking Services LLC

Active Licenses held:

SERIES 6 & 26 (SECURITIES)
LIFE & VARIABLE ANNUITY
PERSONAL LINES (AUTO)
LEGAL
Professional Memberships and Organizations:

E3 Business group/ North Florida and Georgia Chapters
Jacksonville Downtown Business Professionals
The University Club of Jacksonville

I am originally from Houston, Texas and currently reside in
Jacksonville, Florida.

Why I Became a Life Coach?

By Coach Alvin W. King

After spending 20 years working in corporate America, experiencing four lay-offs, coupled with a few life changing events, I decided to take a closer look at what I was living to do. My past experience had been filled with building relationships and managing others. Spreading optimism and positivity to others came natural to me, and I always knew that I wanted to make a difference in the lives of others. I became fascinated with certain talk-show hosts who positively made an impact on their audience.

One day while attending a home-going service of a prominent individual, I listened how others spoke very highly and applauded this individual for the seeds that were planted in the lives of others. I thought to myself at that point, "What would I want others to say about me when I leave this earth?" "What legacy would I want to leave to others?"

I then began to put serious thought into this, and began to recap what some of my strengths were when I was engaging others. I concluded with the fact that beside to being a great listener, I was also an encourager, and a promoter. I always enjoyed "coaching" others; however, I never thought I was actually being a coach!

The greatest pleasure I received was when I was able to assist someone with a major life challenge, and then later receive a report that they had overcame the challenge with a success story.

Through much prayer and meditation, I trusted God to lead me to reach my destiny in becoming a "change agent" for others. I am now excited to embrace infinite opportunities to coach others to reach their destiny in life.

Living without limits!

FISHERS of MEN

And he saith unto them, "follow me and I will make you fishers of men" Matthew 4:19 NKJV

After receiving my Life Coaching certification, I began speaking at various workshops and venues, providing motivational nuggets. My Life Coach Trainer, J. Dianne Tribble asked me about my thoughts on creating a platform for men, whereby I could share my motivation and encouragement. At first I really didn't give it much thought because I was focused on obtaining 20 life coaching clients per month. Then a few months later during a casual conversation, Coach J. Dianne brought this idea up once again.

From the first time she brought it up, I had been approached by several individuals asking me if I coached men and young boys. So this time, I thought to myself, this may be worth more looking into. I then sat down and wrote down a list of the men I knew who I would consider inviting to a men's workshop. Before I knew it, I had over 25 names.

The excitement started to get to me! The Spirit began ministering to me concerning the various topics I would discuss at a men's workshop. My excitement led me to entertaining a name for my men's group. Without referencing any material, I just stopped and asked the Holy Spirit to give me a name for my men's group. Within exactly two minutes, "Fishers of Men" came to me! I had heard of this before in the Bible, however I just knew it was perfect for what I felt God was about to do with me.

I then scheduled my first Fishers of Men workshop in November 2013. I was a great success! To date, I have had several additional workshops.   Fishers of Men evolved into an open discussion platform, whereby men from all walks of life can come together and share experiences, challenges, victories, and gifts with other men.

Fishers of Men is an initiative of Infinite Solutions International. It was the sponsor of the E3 Business Group "Celebrates Fathers" event in downtown Jacksonville, Florida in June 2014.   Fishers of Men has also partnered with Suited for Success to coach, mentor, and prepare men for professional dress for job interviews and new business marketing.

"We seek to be a source for men to learn their true nature in order to solidify their role in society, their place as anchors in our families, and truly understanding their strength through solidarity of purpose."
~ Fishers of Men ~ Coach Alvin W. King

Which GPS Are You Using to Reach Your Destinations in Life?

By Coach Alvin W. King

With the advancement of technology, we all have become reliant on resources to get us where we want to go and get there efficiently. I remember the time when we had to write down directions or use a map to get from one place to another. Then came along MapQuest, where an electronic device did all of the work by knowing our current location and our final destination.

Today we have a GPS tool that can simply take us step by step, mile by mile, to our destination of choice. GPS, which stands for Global Positioning System, is an **"ELECTRONIC"** system that uses satellites to determine the position of a vehicle, person, etc. This device, which audibly speaks your directions in a female or male voice, provides detailed instructions from point A to point B. If you make a wrong turn, it will even recalculate its path or alert you to make a U-turn. This device will also provide you with a choice of getting to your destination with or without traffic by providing detours.

Let me share with you another type of GPS, in which I found also to be helpful in reaching my life's destination. This GPS which stands for **God's Positioning System,** is a **"SPIRITUAL"** system that uses GRACE, DISCERNMENT, TRIALS, FAITH, MERCY,

LOVE, TRIBULATIONS, TRUST, JOY, PEACE, HOPE, FORGIVENESS, PROSPERITY, SUCCESS, TESTIMONIES, ANOINTING, and <u>add yours here</u> to get us to the POSITION where GOD has already designated for us to be. Using our **"SPIRITUAL"** GPS, we can reach our day-to-day mini-destinations in life until we reach our **FINAL DESTINATION** with Christ!

God speaks to you in a small still voice to let you know He is with you along the way. God will tell you, by the Holy Spirit, when you are headed in the wrong direction and there is a need to change your course. You must however, be in the right state of mind and spirit to hear His directions. Align your destiny with God's Positioning System and enjoy your journey!

As a Life Coach, I become a GPS for you as we explore together, where you find yourself in life right now and where you ultimately want to be. We work together to unveil your purpose and your destiny in life. Once you are comfortable with knowing your purpose and having the desire to fulfill it, I coach you through the process of designing your road map required to get there. Keep in mind that at any time you feel the need to change directions or take a detour, I will be there to guide and coach you along the way. I'm confident that you will reach your destiny because I use God's Positioning System. It allows me to be that agent of change in your life and assist you with living life without limits!

FISHERS OF MEN
ENGAGE – EDUCATE – EMPOWER

Coach Alvin W. King
Infinite Solutions International
Fishers of Men
(904) 515-2WIN (2946)
Infinitesolutions1120@gmail.com
www.solutions4life.biz
https://www.facebook.com/pages/Alvin-W-King/323643131094728

My Favorites

Scripture

"Eye has not seen, nor ear heard, nor have entered into the heart of man the things which God has prepared for those who love him" – I Corinthians 2:9 NKJV

Quote

"Faith is taking the first step even when you cannot see the whole staircase". – Dr. Martin Luther King Jr.

Personal Quote

"Work hard and play harder."

~ Coach Alvin W. King

Recommended Reading

"Passing the Tests of Life" (2012)

~ By Bishop George L. Davis

~ Coach Alvin King

Testimonials

Tony Robbins said once "Life is a GIFT and it offers us the privilege, opportunity, and responsibility to give something back by becoming more." This very thought is one of the reason I wanted to affiliate myself with Alvin W. King and the Fishers of Men organization. It allows me to be connected to something bigger than myself. My life has been impacted in so many ways spiritually, physically, socially, emotionally, and financially by each event. Each event has challenged me to dream bigger, charged and inspired to face my obstacles head on, and changed to be the person God has called me to be. I recommend Fishers of Men to anyone who is not pleased with his current circumstances and is looking for ideas of how to change his lifestyle, to the entrepreneur who want to take his business to the next level. I also recommend Fishers of Men to the person who's on the right path, but just need some coaching and accountability to get "across the bridge" from his goals and dreams to success.

~ Marico Walker, Financial Services

Recalling my initial Coaching session with Coach Alvin - After starting the session in prayer, I felt so lifted. I knew it would be a great session. He spoke about what Life Coaching was and jumped right in asking sharp questions about what I was seeking to gain from a Life Coach? He held me very accountable for the action steps in which we discussed in order for me to complete my goals. It was a new experience for me, to be held accountable for what I wanted to accomplish in my life. I am truly grateful that Coach Alvin was available to assist me in getting on the track. After the session, Coach Alvin asked would it be alright if he could check in with me; just to continue to motivate me. I said, "Yes." It is my pleasure to have had an opportunity to be coached by sure a passionate person who loves JESUS CHRIST, who has impacted the lives of others. With what Coach Alvin stands for, he has not seen what GOD is about to do for him in his coaching and everything he touches. His coaching style impacted my life and I thank him because I am still moving forward towards my life goals. Thanks Coach Alvin King. GOD bless you in all you do.

~ Deborah Harvey, Certified Professional Christian Life Coach

That door in your life has closed! Why are you trying to pick the lock?

~ Coach J Dianne Tribble

The Life Coach as a Lighthouse

The role of a Life Coach in the life of a Client, serves as a Lighthouse or beacon. As a Lighthouse, the Life Coach is equipped to provide guidance, instruction, enlightenment, and encouragement as darkness is dispelled. The Life Coach successfully guides the Client in setting, pursuing, and accomplishing goals. The Life Coach does not do the work for the Client. Instead, the Coach provides the support necessary to ensure the expected outcome.

~ Coach J Dianne Tribble

~ Life Story Six ~

Coach Ronline Cannady

My name is Ronline Cannady. I am married; a mother of an adult son; godmother to several god-children; and I am a native Floridian. A few years ago, I was ordained as minister, under the leadership of Reverend M. Newell, pastor of White Dove Holiness Church in Jacksonville, Florida. I am excited about having earned my training/coaching certification this year and doubly excited about my newfound calling as a business, career, and Christian Life Coach (which has taken me on a journey of great spiritual rewards). I have been afforded the opportunity to work with many Christian leaders. As a result, I have gained greater insight about leadership and stewardship. I coach people to embrace their niche and start a new phase in their lives - just as I have done.

VIP

(VICTORIOUS IN PRAYER)

By Coach Ronline Cannady

Have you ever observed an athletic coach in action when he is running down the court, around the track, overseeing the laps of the swimmer, or on the field?   Did you feel the energy, the excitement, the emotion, or disappointment from the coach?

I can relate. The coach wants the athlete to win. What is winning? Winning is to be successful at whatever the task may be. I also define it as the victorious moment over my battle of defeat.

I had to personally overcome many battles that brought about defeat because of being in bondage of some type. I found out over time how to be victorious over the defeat. I had to learn how to pray. In time, I found that my grandparents, parents, ministers, friends and family were all correct. There truly is power in prayer. There is an acronym for the word PUSH that people like to use for the act of praying. It stands for "pray until something happens."

I have witnessed many testimonies from my personal clients as a result of prayer. Many of my clients come to me broken in spirit for one reason or another, but after a few sessions they are ready to take on the world's challenges and climb the higher hill and mountains to reach their goals.

My Story

Over three years ago, I placed myself on notice for a period of 1,000 days. While at a Toastmasters meeting, one of the speakers, Valerie Baham, spoke about a man who purchased 1,000 marbles. Each marble represented one Saturday. He decided that he would do something special each Saturday until he had reached the end of his marbles. This story alone, spoke volumes to me. I was tired of being directionless. I had always accommodated others and never thought about using the life that God had given me for myself.

After discussing my concerns with my husband, I made a list of 30 things that I needed to complete or do. Within the first 17 days, more than half the items on the list were completed. Each year was filled with satisfying accomplishments, and now I am addicted. I have signed up for the second round of the 1,000-day challenge. Coaching was added to the list this year, and I have my certifications to coach and to assist in training new trainees for the certification coaching program offered by At the Table Life Coaching & Motivational Speaking services LLC.

I am rewarded when I see clients smiling and laughing again. It exhilarates and refreshes my soul. For this reason alone, I enjoy coaching. When a person is held accountable for his/ her own agenda, he/ she will do whatever it takes to get things done, and a newfound power emerges. It's like the butterfly emerging from its chrysalis and its wings have to fill up with fluid called the hemolymph before it can spread its wings and fly. This is similar to blood running through human veins and causing people to do amazing things with their limbs.

The chrysalis is a wonderful place to be during transformation from the old self into the new self. You begin to believe in yourself, and you lay aside everything that held you in captivity.

Think about the captivity that you are in for a moment. Aren't there things in your life that you would like to be free of? Becoming a Christian Life Coach ushered me into a freedom of ministry. My parishioners can leave their religious masks at home and reveal the real persons inside. They shed the skin of pain and walk into the newness of life. People want to feel the joys of life. I know I did, and that is what makes this coaching process so powerful for me - it truly humbles me each time one of my clients receive a breakthrough. Each time a client breaks the chains; my heart opens and exposes the true heart of a Christian Coach.

Our Savior, Jesus Christ, demonstrated that we must master expressing love for people. When we have love for people, our heart fills up with love and resembles the heart of a Coach.

In having the heart of a Coach, you will embrace your Clients, encourage them, support them, and give them the love they need in order to grow. At the same time, I show the "tough love" they need in order to stay accountable. As Clients achieve their goals, the rewards have the potential to get larger and larger. Some of my Clients have headed into new directions and left behind things that no longer mattered. They strive to become better in accomplishing things they felt they lacked the ability to achieve.

Observing life emerging in my clients, brings a bittersweet emotion for both me and them. The best example that I can provide is this: If your loved one experiences a traumatic accident and the prognosis looks bleak, you prepare yourself to do whatever you can to accommodate that person in establishing a new normalcy. Then a miracle happens. Your loved one requests a full course meal and stands ready to walk out of the hospital without even one day of therapy. Life emerges. Joy takes over the soul. Joy takes over me when I am coaching my clients and they have their "ah-ha" moments.

My trainer for the coaching certification program wrote a book entitled, *"The Star Inside of You: Motivational Nuggets and Inspirational Stories of Encouragement."* Through this process, I have learned that in order for people to trust God with everything, you have to demonstrate in your own life that you trust God with everything.

I have learned that I really don't know my client, even if we have a long history of friendship. Dissatisfied people realize that they need to do something because they are tired of traveling in the labyrinth with no results, so they try the Coaching approach.

During the initial and subsequent coaching sessions, their self-confidence soars because of accomplishments they may achieve in a relatively short time span.   Real issues come forth and excitement takes over. It is during this time that I am introduced to the real person trapped within. Many people commit to being coached then back off because of shame and embarrassment.   Once the real person appears and makes a bold statement, the real work of Christian coaching begins.

As a Christian Life Coach,   I get so filled when my clients, of all ages, stand firm on the decision to accept Jesus Christ in their lives and study the Word of God. My heart fills with joy and excitement because I am looking for the lessons that God brings forth in His movement to save His people from perishing.

Not every client that I Coach accepts Jesus Christ. As a Coach I pray over their lives, but with a different approach. As a minister, I pray with them and over them and their loved ones' lives. I remind clients of a few biblical demonstrations, and then I make them aware that they are breathing the breath of life – a gift from God. I remind them that I stand in prayer for them and their safety with the acceptance of God's blueprint for our lives. I remind them that no matter what area they prefer to receive Coaching (whether in business, career, finance, or salvation), it becomes an opportunity to serve for God. I look forward to God removing shame and sin from their lives and replacing it with divine joy while performing spiritual surgery on their hearts so they can embrace God's love.

As a Life Coach and a follower of God's teaching, I want to touch and agree with all of the potential Life Coaches that you will find yourself with a deeper yearning to be as one with God and understanding the many uses that he has for each of us to reach His people. I want our lives to align up with the plan that he had envisioned for each of us to fulfill. I pray that you will do as I did and take the challenge to place yourself on notice to get your life aligned with God's order.

Do you have that desire for people? Do you feel a burning desire in yourself to allow yourself to come alive and be there for others? That is what happened to me. I had a burning desire to be there for people that were giving up and wanted to exit this world, oftentimes without a trace of being remembered by anyone. I knew what that place of void looked and felt like. I wanted to provide meaning into the lives of others, and I never knew how to remove the feeling of void from me.

One day I discovered Christian Life Coaching, and while in the process of being coached, I realized that the emptiness that I felt previously did not exist any longer. I found out that as your love for God grows, the more empty spaces are filled with his everlasting joy. My heart became so large for the love of God, to the point that I wanted to give back by providing others with what was given and shared with me.

May God bless your life richly with His loving Spirit and tender mercies. May you find your place in the ministry of God's will.

~ Coach Ronline Cannady

What is a Life Coach?

By Coach Ronline Cannady

A Life Coach is someone who has taken an oath to assist others in reaching their goals of making positive changes in their lives. This is accomplished by the Coach through training in leadership and discipleship. A Coach must be willing to serve in the capacity of planting the seeds of motivation through testimony (unmasking himself/herself and become transparent to the Client), providing a safe and confidential environment for the Client to unmask and become transparent), show support by using the strength within to allow the Client to overcome challenges that causes discouragement and despair, respect to the Client's revelations and goals and most importantly of all, keep your client accountable for his or her actions. When you keep your Client accountable, your Client will be willing to overcome barriers and embrace change. God gave us a brief demonstration of that with Adam and Eve (Genesis 3:11-19). God not only strengthened them to withstand the life they had to lead, that was clearly out of his will, but He equipped them and gave them expectations to be able to earn their way back to Him again.

As Coaches, we must be obedient to the Word of God and respect God' alignment of order in which He has prepared for our lives. As Coaches, I feel we are charged with the responsibility to live the lives of leaders and be ready to assist our Clients, Coaches, ministries, etc, to live the lives of leaders - ready to lead and train others to use their spiritual gifts to strengthen others and allow them to transform to the beauty which is within (waiting to be unleashed).

The life that Jesus led with his disciples is a perfect example in which Life Coaches can emulate. Jesus took on an oath to come to teach those of us that would believe that we can have eternal life.

I believe that a Christian Life Coach should take on a similar oath, to bring a realization that a Client can choose better options for himself/herself. Jesus has made it possible to have a life change or a paradigm shift, from the way a Client was doing things to bringing him/her into a place to "reset" for a new beginning.

The Coaching approach can position you for a lifetime transformation of permanent and positive change. Once the Client has made that pivotal point around God's center, he/she normally never want to return to the former person.

Some people have tried to return to the former person and some succeeded. Some did not dwell there very long, because when they experienced being whole; being centered; and being aligned with the Word of God, they immediately began to feel an opened-emptiness that only God's glory could fulfill.

Can anyone be a Coach? If you have the love of God in

your heart and soul, you will most likely find yourself in some form of Coaching. Matthew 22:36-40 explains the greatest commandments in all of his laws, the love of people. If you have the love of people then you will develop the love of God in greater depths. 2 Peter 3:9 speaks volumes about God's promises. It is not his wish that we should perish. Perishing and not gain eternal life is not a part of God's plan.

We were given free will to make choices concerning the path we want to follow. There are times in our lives when we come upon the crossroads and we need to select the road that is less traveled. We want to be labeled as the faithful laborers and we all must realize that the road that leads to God has a few travelers. We want to be in the number of the few. We want to develop the heart of David, Moses, and Jesus in order to set our goals to reach the higher levels which were promised to us.

Jesus so often demonstrated how we can be steadfast and unmovable in our faith. As a Coach, it is important to be steadfast and unmovable with our clients. Clients depend on the Coach to be the solid rock of encouragement, to bring them through the uncertainties of life.

A Life Coach provides a safe environment for a Client to unmask, accept who he/she is, provide encouragement, give the Client quality time, and finally, provide the support the Client needs in order to set goals. The Client will transform from being a rough stone to being a smooth and polished stone.

Remember the story about how David, the simple shepherd boy, brought down the terrors of Goliath with five smooth stones? Likewise, the Life Coach in the life of a Client allows him/her the freedom and support to bring down many of the "Goliaths" in his/her life. Some Coaches go as far as climbing the highest mountain with their Clients by climbing from the other side, and meeting them at the top. A Life Coach will be in that role of support all the way, yet will give the client the distance or space needed in order to accomplish the goals.

A Life Coach provides a place of "reset" in order for a client to get unstuck. At that point, a client can enjoy a life that is full of meaning and purpose.

~ *Coach Ronline Cannady*

Case Studies

My first client, Ms. Monique Freeney of Jacksonville, Florida, was the toughest, yet I enjoyed working with her. She helped me to sharpen my coaching skills and challenged me to ask the tough questions as I kept her accountable. By the fourth session, we were both transformed. You see, God was holding both of us accountable. Monique realized that she could do whatever she set her mind to do and I realized that the challenges while coaching need not break me, but embolden me. Monique sought God's help in planning and achieving her goals. As a result, she started completing her goals. "You did it Monique!" I look forward to working with you in the near future on your next set of goals.

My second client, Jerry Lightner, Jr. lives in Chicago, Illinois. This young man, who was in his last semester of college, faced financial hardship and difficult decisions. While establishing his agenda for completing school, he added additional goals which would boost his chances for landing a career opportunity. Jerry satisfied his financial obligations, graduated with honors, and made great career choices. Today, he is doing great work with videography and more. It was wonderful working with Jerry.

In my coaching studies, I've learned that every situation can be a great coaching opportunity. I am a member of a local Toastmasters-Lillian R. Bradley # 2346. During one of our meetings, Karen Pollard, a young woman bursting with full life and energy, told me she envisioned herself as a motivational speaker.

She desperately wanted to be voted as the best speaker whenever she gave speeches. During one of her presentations, she remained focused, overcame all of her usual distractions, and delivered her speech with absolute authority. Karen was voted the best speaker. She said, "I found out I was stronger and believed in myself, and I felt honored to be voted as the best speaker amongst the seasoned competitors." As her Coach, I too, was honored.

Remember my Client Jerry? He was faced with all kinds of adversary in his last semester. He was at the point of giving up. As he continued his journey through the Coaching process, he learned that he made many sacrifices to continue his education. The Coaching process brought him to a place in his life whereby he was able to look at himself. He realized that he is his greatest asset, and he has the ability to take control of his circumstances. He won! He was victorious! He felt good!

Karen did the same thing. She focused on what she wanted. She realized she was competing with seasoned speakers, but she persevered. She is now ready to proceed to the hard work that awaits her. That is exactly what all of us must do, persevere and proceed to what is ahead of us.

Monique, my toughest Client, likes having a place of security, where she can bring forth issues that would hinder her walk with God. She encourages me, on so many levels, to keep the ministry of Coaching at the forefront because people are more aware of their issues and shortcomings than they care to admit. When the woman was about to be stoned to death for her adulterous lifestyle, Jesus didn't leave her. He gave a command to the people judging her and knelt down to draw on the ground. He demonstrates that He will never leave nor forsaken you. He is with you even though you can't see Him. He may not provide an answer for you at the very moment you need one, but He is always present and on time.

Free yourself from shame, guilt and anything that prevents you from being unleashed. Moreover, when Jesus asked the Samarian woman to draw Him some water. He didn't discriminate against her for living an undesirable lifestyle and having multiple husbands. He simply asked her if she would like to exchange the regular water to the everlasting water that springs forth and quenches thirst forever.

Remember that God accepts us where we are. We only need to say, "Yes!" to the call and obedience of God. Accept His precious Son, Jesus Christ in your life and live out the teachings and demonstrations He shared with us from His Father.

Take control of your life. Embrace your life for restoration, starting today. Find a Bible-believing church and a Christian Coach so that you can remain accountable. If you don't know any Coaches, contact At the Table Life Coaching (www.atthetableinc.com). We are always ready to serve and give you the support you need. If our great and awesome God is our Jehovah Jireh, Jehovah Rapha, Jehovah Nissi and Jehovah Shalom, then trust Him that He who made you knows all about you and will receive you right now. May God bless and keep you.

Coach J. Dianne Tribble, keep allowing the stars to arise in you and all of your coaches. We need you. Keep allowing God to direct your path. Thank you for all that you have poured into us with your prayers, love and longsuffering.

My plans for the future include a project about the butterfly emerging from the chrysalis. Please pray for me and all of my Coaches. They have each set a foundation within me to bring the chrysalis movement forward. May the love of God dwell and rise with you as it blesses you abundantly.

I must give thanks to my son, my husband, mother and family for all of their continued support throughout my growth. They all have kept me accountable in countless capacities.

I leave one message with you. One of my Coaches, Demetrice Elaine Vassar, taught me to seek and shine. I am passing this torch to you. In all your ways seek God and allow his precious Spirit to shine through you, so that you will be a lighthouse for someone who has lost their way. Thanks D., I love you always.

~ Coach Ronline Cannady

Coaching Evaluation with Client

By Coach Ronline Cannady and Client

As a coaching client, what did you fine most helpful to you in the process?
I indeed found coaching helpful because it helped me to be verbally vocal, and to identify my strengths as well as weaknesses, and to be comfortable all at the same time.

How do you feel the coaching process can assist others?
It can assist others in a positive way by creating a better understanding of the overall one –on- one teaching.

Do you feel the experience assist you with your walk with God? If so, explain.
Absolutely. It's taught me growth, and the mirror reflections of who I am on the outside as well as on the inside. I've learned how to maintain a strategic plan on how to set futuristic goals by planning the work and working the plan.

What is your overall feeling about the strategy that your Coach used in the coaching process?
Honestly, it's a joyous feeling. Coach Ronline Cannady demonstrated the overall plan to benefit my needs, in a more dynamic approach. She was concerned, compassionate, but very straight forward to the point. She truly has a genuine heart for God's people.

Anything you want to share with the readers about your Coach?
I recommend her to anyone with one-on-one needs, ones that are struggling to know their inner selves, or ones that just need a person to listen. Coach Ronline Cannady is by far, the best mentor who I feel has touched my life in unexplainable ways, and I know others will be Blessed by her Wisdom, and knowledge.

My Favorites

Quote

"I've learned that people will forget what you said, people will forget what you did, but people will never forget how you made them feel."

Maya Angelou

Quote

"Don't just leave, plan to leave."

Evangelist Martina Newell

Quote

"You are going to respect me for having respect for you."

Jerome Q. L. Newell

"Out of the minutes that God blesses us in a day, take a few minutes to encourage a stranger. Your encouragement may cause the stranger to get back into the game and do something great." ~ Coach Ronline

~ Coach Ronline Cannady

Testimonial

Authority, such a misunderstood term...disliked, in some instances detested. However, a woman of authority, divine authority, is a commodity to have in one's corner. Ronline walks in an authority that places her in a position of personal hierachy with an essence of virtue. She gracefully speaks with authority and whatever she speaks, she follows through meticulously.

I would watch from a distance, her involvement with others. Ronline desires for people to do better, to reach beyond the break, to have people know that there is greater within one's self and all one has to do is look deep within to find a speck of determination and act therein upon it. She references the divine power that everything is moving by and encourages a soul to press forward, as all circumstances are temporary at best. She searches for the best in people who only see the worst in themselves and provides a brighter self-examination that exhumes a light in what seems to be the darkest of situations.

After witnessing her genuine zeal for people, I then made myself known to her. I was in a shell of self hatred not understanding why I suffered the way I did. Not wanting to be up front or noticed, not wanting to be Beautiful because that's what seemed to lead to abuse by other's which sparked self abuse. Ronline saw what I didn't have to say. In spite of all that had happened to me she reminded me that I wasn't a victim.....I was a survivor. She encouraged me to speak out and to further my education. I take no glory from God as He deserves it all, but it would be a heinous error to not give credit where credit is due. If it had not been for her countless, unwavering pursuit in my success, I wouldn't be an installed Apostle, neither would I had obtained the Medical Billing degree.

I believe there are people specifically designed to encourage. In a world of contempt, hatred, malice, jealousy, etc....it is nothing short of a miracle to have that one person, to know everything about you but not hold it against you. But have you, instead of seeing stumbling blocks as hindrances, use the block to step up and become greater. Ronline is that one person.......a virtuous, determined woman of authority.

~ Apostle Valencia Brown-Walker of Jacksonville, Florida

Coach Ronline Cannady's Contact Information

Business Name: Coach RONCAN Life Coaching Services

Business line: 904-357-0840

Email address: ProfcoachRon_can@aol.com

> ***Even the Encourager needs encouragement.***
> ***~ Coach J Dianne Tribble***

~ **Life Story Seven** ~

Coach Gina Jackson

Coach Gina Jackson is a Memphis native, born and raised in Orange Mound TN, to Gail Smith and the late Billy McGee. Gina grew up in a single parent household with two of her five siblings. The only girl, Coach Gina grew up being no stranger to homemaking. She filled in as her mother worked two or more jobs in order to provide for her and her siblings. Her mother was a big advocate in the community, where she sat on the Board of Collaboration for the community in which they lived most of Coach Gina's childhood. This is where Coach Gina believes she developed a passion for people. In 2009 Coach Gina married Frederick Jackson. Early in 2010, her husband accepted naval orders to relocate to Jacksonville FL, where they currently reside.

She confessed Christ early in life around the age of 6 at Hickory Hill Baptist Church in Memphis TN.. Coach Gina is now a Certified Life Coach and a motivational and inspirational speaker for women and teens. She strives to empower women all over the world. Coach Gina is currently looking to raise suicide awareness and to lead discussions around death in the black community. She is determined to educate parents and guardians on how to discuss difficult topics with their children. Coach Gina volunteers for PACE Center for Girls (a high-risk girls' school in Jacksonville, FL) and Junior Achievement as an instructor.

Gina is the founder of "Her Integrated Truth Coaching." She is currently pursuing her BA in Business Management at California Career Coast University. She is also a fulltime retirement representative for a fortune 500 financial firm.

This Is My Story

I am Christian Life Coach Gina Jackson. I came to Jacksonville, Florida not knowing what to do with my life or how to identify what my responsibilities were, or what didn't fall under my responsibilities. I just knew I was happy to be out of Memphis, which was my childhood dream. I just wanted to make it out. At that moment I was so happy not to be a statistic. I never knew what it would take or how I would end up where I am today. I had no guide on what "walking by faith and not by sight" consisted of. Oh, but God! Come take a walk with me, now this Life Coach, founder and CEO of Integrated Truth Coaching, where you will see how God took my wrongs and made them right and is still blowing my mind up until this day.

In September of 2013, I was still overjoyed with God's mercy and unknown plans for my life. While at work one day, I recall a co-worker walking up to me and asking me why I was always smiling. Thinking to myself, "She has no idea how long I prayed to get out of Memphis." I then replied, GRINNING FROM EAR TO EAR, "I just am."

She then laughed and shook her head and asked me to join her and a few of our coworkers in accompanying them in a women's luncheon downstairs. I replied, "No thanks" as always. She then said, "You never come to anything. Come on. They will have food."

I am not a big eater, but I felt convicted at that moment. I was thinking, "I never attend anything. What's the harm in attending?"

I remember sitting down in a conference room full of diverse women from all walks of life. I was then introduced to Coach J Dianne Tribble, CEO of At the Table Life Coaching Services. As I sat there, she was opening her presentation with an ice breaker. I was so in tuned and "all ears" because everything she saying was what I was experiencing or what I had experienced before in my prior life. I became overjoyed with water works (tears) and confirmation that God had heard my most intimate prayers. I immediately signed up for her Coaching class after her presentation.

I called her right after my shift but she didn't answer. I left her a message telling her who I was, but a part of the old me, who was filled with all types of fear and doubt didn't believe she was going to call me back. Later that night she returned my call. I was so excited when she did. I told her to sign me up for her next available class. The rest is history for now.

Well this is how I became A LIFE COACH. The "why factor" hadn't been answered yet. Let's keep walking and see how God brought me into my purpose driven life as a Life Coach.

A few weeks later I started my first Coach training session. During the session, I recall Coach J Dianne asking me, "What are your plans for your Life Coach certification?" At that time, I could hear birds chirping. I had no idea at that time what God's purpose was for my life and now, I was adding a certification to the mix! I couldn't answer the question honestly. I then heard the sound of crickets.

At the end of the session that night, I thought about it once or twice but shunned it off. I went into prayer mode posing the same question she asked me, to God. I heard crickets and birds chirping again. I thought about it and thought about it over and over. I hadn't received any response. I just went to bed. The next day it was still on my mind. I began to question my faith and God. I was wondering if he was going to answer her question for me. I felt so overwhelmed because I was taught "you always have a plan for a plan and never be caught without a plan."

At that time, I didn't know that God was testing me. I have learned during my transition that God does not operate on an earthly schedule. I later realized the type of life I was accustomed to living before, left no room for God. This is why I believe God tells us when you are married, you are to cling to your spouse and leave your family. You are a child far longer than an adult for some of us. You have to learn to discern what is His will for your life and what is man's fear pressed upon your life.

Again I was speechless. I had to ask myself, "You have asked God what He wanted you to do with your certification, right?" As I thought back, I had to ask myself that question over and over but I still did not have a confident answer. This was very unusual for me. I always have an answer, a thought or something in mind. So later that night I addressed the same question she asked me to God again. I asked him to lead me and guide me in the way in which He wanted me to use my certification. I had no idea how God was about to shift my life and test my faith.

That night I went to bed puzzled. I had to repent and pray harder as I waited. I had to repent because I was beginning to revert back to my old ways of becoming fearful and doubtful. I have had so much experience doing things this way. I couldn't say, "I apologize" fast enough and repent. I was sure I was not going to make the same mistake again.

I have experienced God "showing up and out" throughout my life, as well as now. I could wait a little while longer. He does have a 100% turnover rate. I remember God reminding me not to be as hard on myself as I often am. He reminded me that this way of thinking isn't something I just started. This has been my way of living, thinking, and doing things for years. I had to undo it in order to walk with Him.

Afterwards, I had a clear picture of the transition I was experiencing. I also then understood that this was true for everyone else as well. Everyone at some point will go through this transition. It's a place where you are left making a decision between the way you did things in the past and embracing God's future plans for you. I just thank God I am conscious of my actions. I check myself and correct myself, all at the same time. I am my worst critic. You have to remember, I didn't just develop this way of thinking yesterday. I have been questioning God and myself, not trusting in anyone, for years. What's your excuse? Let's just keep walking. It's is easier than taking responsibility or self-preservation.

So a month or two later passed after J Dianne formed what seemed like a million dollar question. As I was preparing to take the final exam, I was still drawing a blank as to what God's plans were for me as a Coach. I then said to God, "You know I am still waiting on you." He replied, "Yep I know." I said to Him, "It's getting close, really close to my final exam, you know. What are you going to do, wait until the day of?" He didn't reply. I continued to wait. I began to overlook the pressure I was feeling about not having the answer for myself and Coach J Dianne.

As the week for my final testing slowly approached, I received more than my answer. I received heart wrenching information from my grandmother that my brother was in ICU and she had no idea if he was going to make it. Later that day I had to call Coach J Dianne to tell her I was not going to be able to take my final exam. I had to prepare myself to go home to bury my brother. My life had suffered a major loss, and fast. Not until I was responding to another one of Coach J Dianne's thought-provoking questions, did it dawn on me that God had giving me the answer to the first question. Yes, God gave me my answer in the result of the death of my brother. I was devastated once again.

I learned during my brother's transition, how to remain in faith and confidence in God during the most unforeseen, disruptive, and hurtful times in your life. Prior to losing my brother, I would have turned into "someone else." I now understand why it is so important to keep God first and to maintain a balance in life. God unveiled my gift and potential while revealing what is now my little brother's past life. God gave me peace and understanding about the suicidal death of my 23 year old brother. Amazing. I know. Unpredictable. That's the God I serve.

It's difficult to understand, but my brother lived a full life, greater than statistics show for someone his age coming out of Memphis, and more than most of our adult relatives which were twice his age. See I may not understand everything that comes my way, but what I know is this; God never left me. I know my brother was tired of experiencing man's disappointments, but I say to anyone thinking suicidal thoughts, "Keep on pressing forward and don't give up on God. Maintain your faith in Him and your unforeseen dreams and desires."

As a child, I also experienced suicidal and demonized thoughts, BUT GOD! You too can make it. I DID and you can too.

During the summer of 2002, my other three brothers and I were faced with what marked the hardest point in our lives. Our father was murdered in his North Memphis home by his friend. As children, we had no idea how to grieve or how to pick up the pieces of our lives after losing a person that was so dear to us. I was trying to balance it all, as everything was crumbling before my eyes quicker than I could put my hands together to catch the pieces of my life. As the oldest sister of these three, I had no idea what to do for the first time in my life. At home with my mom, I had to grieve fast and get back to being the responsible teen.

After many mistakes, adversities and failed relationships, I had had enough. I was tired and ready to give up on my life, my city, and my family. I was ready for a change. I had no idea how God was about to transition my life. After a long talk with God, I asked Him to remove people, circumstances and situations, if they or it wasn't in line with what He had planned for my life.

Shortly after that I met my now husband of five years. After a short period of dating, we got married. He joined the military and we moved to Jacksonville FL.

Presently, I volunteer with adolescents at PACE Center for Girls, a high-risk girls' school, and Junior Achievement for Girls. I have written a business proposal, establishing a foundation to be an advocate for grieving children.

In loving Memory of Jermey S. Graham

July 15, 1990 to Dec 13, 2013

~ Coach Gina Jackson

My Personal Testimony

I have died here on earth but God has given me a second chance. HE has afforded me the opportunity to pursue my gifts and many talents. I have chosen to go after my gifts...... which one will you choose?

In every desire of my heart and for every unanswered question I have ever had, God has given me clarity and confirmation, which has given me the understanding of how to move on.

I had to redo, undo and repair all areas of my life and it wasn't easy but God carried me over.

I had to forgive in order to be forgiven.

God helped me to mend my relationship with my Mom and gave me the role of being her cheerleader in her time of need and aspiration.

~ Coach Gina Jackson

My Favorites

Scripture

Do not judge others, and you will not be judged. Do not condemn others, or it will all come back against you. Forgive others, and you will be forgiven.
~ Luke 6:37

Pursing your talent given by God comes with a price paid by the individual, pursing your gift given by God produces revenue for the individual. By: ~
~Coach Gina Jackson

Scripture

"If you forgive those who sin against you, your heavenly Father will forgive you."
~ Matthew 6:14

Personal Quote

"Aspire to be the ultimate woman whom is well rounded spiritually, physically and mentally."
~ Coach Gina Jackson

~ Coach Gina Jackson

Testimonials

I remember confiding in Gina about my fear of sharing something painful and personal with my loved ones. The first thing she said was "Let me know how much the plane ticket is and tell me when I have to take off from work." I laughed, but her face was serious. She said, "Whatever you're holding on to is hurting you and if you don't address it, that pain will consume you."

I won't forget what she said, *ever*. These words truly resonated with me. She challenged me to take a look within myself and acknowledge those fears.

The thing about Gina is, she's not afraid to live her truth. Her willingness to be so open and honest helps others recognize that they have the ability to do the same. There is so much power in living your truth; but when you bury your truth, it has power over you. She saw that happening to me. For that, I'm eternally thankful. In a way, she saved me from who I could've become. Letting that pain fester was so destructive to my growth.

It goes without question that Gina is selfless, genuine and rare. She's someone who's not afraid to invest in herself. She knows that "to change the world, you must change yourself." A friendship with her is pure quality. She's the type of friend to pray with you in the middle of a crowded restaurant; the type of friend to follow through on a commitment, even when sick; the type of friend who is always there to uplift and encourage; the type of friend who will support you consistently; and the type of friend with enough drive and passion for 10 people. That tenacity- that power- is what inspires me to become a better version of myself.

~ Ashley Salliey, Navy Wife

Throughout this Coaching experience journey, I have witnessed Gina turn into an amazing woman and person. She has not only transformed and changed herself, but she has helped me as well. She has been encouraging, supportive and has helped me to see the best in me so that I may be able to see the best in others. Just like 5+5 is 10 and 9+1 also gets 10, she has shown me that there is more than one way to view life and not everyone sees it as I do. We all have one true common focus in life and that's to be happy and find our true calling and purpose in life. I truly admire her and will forever be grateful for helping me to focus and take into perspective what my purpose in life is!!!! ~

Katrena Patrick, Navy Wife

~ Coach Gina Jackson

Top Recommended Reading List

1. <u>Discerning the Voice of God</u> by Priscilla Shirer (2012)
2. <u>Living Your Best Life Now</u> by Joel Osteen (2004)
3. <u>The Purpose Drive Life</u> by Rick Warren (2007)
4. <u>More Than Enough</u> by Dave Ramsey (2002)
5. <u>The Total Money Makeover</u> by Dave Ramsey (2013)
6. <u>Leadership Coaching: The Disciplines, Skills and Heart of a Christian Coach</u> by Tony Stoltzfus (2005)

Are you wasting time on the "Yellow Brick Road?"
Follow the Way, the Truth, & the Light.
Time is of the essence.
~ Coach J Dianne Tribble

~ Life Story Eight ~

Coach Cindy Coates

My name is Cindy Coates, I was born and raised in Baltimore Md. I have two adult sons, Rob 33 and Jason 31. I attended college in Maryland. I received a degree in Psychology and completed studies in Social Work and I minored in Counseling Psychology. Some of my core studies were Marriage and Family, Eating Behaviors, Psychology of Learning and Culture, and Psychology of Anger and Aggression, I also completed some graduate classes in Gender and Aging issues. I have worked for several large hospitals both in Baltimore, Maryland and Jacksonville, Florida. I am a member of Celebration Church and I am blessed to be pastored by Pastors Stovall and Kerri Weems. I serve in Guest Services, Sisterhood Women's Ministry, and I lead an outreach ministry at the local Mental Health Hospital. I serve as a group leader and facilitator for Celebrate Recovery, a ministry of Chetts Creek Church.

My community volunteer work covers many areas: Mental Health Advocacy, Community Emergency Response Team (CERT), Red Cross Emergency Shelter Operator, and Trauma intervention.

I have certifications in the Work Net Program, Disability Resources, and training with NAMI (National Alliance of Mental Illness).

I am a photographer. My work has been featured with the Jacksonville Chamber of Commerce and also in Advantage Magazine. I have done volunteer photography for many non-profit organizations such as Best Buddies, Girls on the Run, Sulzbacher Sisterhood Outreach, One Spark, and many other events throughout Northeast Florida. I began my photography business, Moooving Moments Photography, in Dec 2008.

In 2009, I became the assistant organizer for a large networking group in Jacksonville, FL called Network4FreeNJax. I co-facilitated weekly meetings to bring awareness to business owners and I also led discussions on improving business networking. During my time as a networking leader, I developed my passion for connecting people. The basic formula for a successful connection is to get to know the person, allow them to get to know you, and establish trust. As humans, we are wired to connect with people; which is imperative in the life experience. A very important point is to concentrate of giving rather than receiving. As author of "The Go Giver," Bob Burg states, "People must know, like and trust us before they do business with us. Don't be a go getter, be a Go Giver."

My goal currently is to build a community resource network through a group of people which I have named W.A.V.E. This stands for We Are Vision Empowered. God planted this vision in my heart in 2007, to begin a group where people with common values, but diverse backgrounds could come together to dream, vision and empower others in the community to do something that is bigger than themselves. We are establishing W.A.V.E. as a Networking Group. We have a vision of opening a co-op facility where business owners may work together and share resources as they give back to the community with their gifts and talents.

As a Life Coach, I feel I'm adding more tools in my belt. I am creating my job title of Customer Relationship Manager, Business Vision Consultant, and Social Network Connector.

My goal is to help you become the best person that you were born to be.
~ Coach Cindy Coates

Stepping Into the Waves

As I walked by the ocean, I saw many shells. The waves crashed on the shore and tossed the shells around. Some were broken and dirty, some were beautiful and shiny. I lifted the shell from its sandy home and gave it care and love. I took it home and gave it a purpose. Just like Jesus is with us through the storms of our lives, He picks us up broken and worn out. He places us in His hands and He begins to shape us into a beautiful creation.

There is a time for every season under Heaven. Ecclesiastes 3:8 talks about this - a time to sow, a time to water and watch, a time to reap, and a time to rest. Green equals to growth. Growth is something that we all go through. If you are comfortable, then you are probably not growing. One of my favorite quotes from H. Jackson Browne states, "Don't be afraid to step out on a limb. That's where the fruit is."

Ever since I was around 33 years old, I knew God had given me the gift of making connections with people. My younger years were quite different, I was an only child who was sheltered and kept very safe and secure. I was insecure, awkwardly shy, and completely unable to have a conversation with anyone. I was afraid of my own shadow. I can remember clinging to my Mother's dress on the first day of kindergarten, thinking that I was being pulled away from the security of my Mom.

Years went by. I progressed through school, through

marriage, and then on to motherhood. This was the time in my life which caused a big turn for the better. When you are a Mom, you will do anything, go anywhere and say anything to protect your children.

As I look at my life up to this point in time, I know that I have been through many trials and tribulations. I have looked at the ground covered with weeds. I have tilled the ground. I have planted seeds in the ground and I have thrown seeds to the wind. I have been in darkness and I have been in light. I have been in the parched sun and the torrential downpour.

I realize that I must be like a tree that is ever reaching up to the sun. As the limbs grow upward, some of them become crowded out. They choke and die due to lack of sun. They wither due to lack of rain. Sometimes the limbs of our tree are torn down by natural disasters such as hurricanes or from natural or man-made fire.

Out of the ashes we look around and see what we have left. We strengthen our supports and set out again to plant new seedlings. We may do this over and over throughout our lifetimes. Some of these trees were never meant to take root. Some people don't see the potential in a seed. You may choose to look at it as a speck or see it as an orchard. It is all your perspective. God will direct the sun and the water to care for the visions He has for our lives.

As I reflect on the seasons of my life, I realize that everything that I have accomplished and all the difficulties I have overcome have allowed me to walk into this season of life where I am now. I am humbled by the light that shines through me to draw others towards Him. I was led by God to be a connector, a nurturer, a counselor, and a caretaker.

Through each of these chapters, I have learned many important life lessons. My first chapter was Motherhood, which I absolutely adored; however, at times I did not feel as if I had all the skills I needed. So I sought counseling and education. Before my oldest son turned two, my Mother at the age of 58 was diagnosed with Stage 4 Ovarian Cancer. She went through major abdominal surgery and 16 months of Chemotherapy. I was caring for my young son and was the caretaker for my Mom. We had just bought our first home. Mother needed constant care and God allowed me to be with her throughout her illness. We rented out our house and moved in to my parents' home.

My Mom succumbed to cancer in Oct 1983. That same year, I found out I was pregnant with our second son. I was very sick. God gave me the strength I needed to endure the loss of my mother. I feel He gave me a new baby to help me heal from the loss of my mother.

I adored being a stay at home Mom. We finally moved out of my parents' house and into a townhouse. There I began to feel like I could live as an adult and raise my children.

Not long after that move, my Dad was diagnosed with lung cancer and had to have a lung removed. He was living alone, so we moved him in with us. We made him a nice little room in the basement of the townhouse. We put up walls so he could have privacy. There he recuperated and was surrounded by his grandsons whom he adored.

The boys were five and two years of age. Unexpectedly, my Mother's Mom, who was 90 years old, suffered a heart attack. She went to the hospital and it was determined that she could no longer live alone in her house. We moved our boys into the same bedroom and gave my Grandmother the third bedroom. This was a very challenging time in my life.

I had two young sons, and my Dad and my Grandmother both recuperating under the same roof. To top it off, they were never able to see eye to eye. There were times when I really didn't know how I was going to make it through the day. Sometimes I would just fall into bed and collapse from exhaustion.

It was during those times that I would think about the poem "Footprints in the Sand" by Mary Stevenson. When the man was on the beach and only saw one set of footprints, he cried out to Jesus and said, "If you are here with me, why don't I see your footprints?" It was then that Jesus said, "That time son, was when I was carrying you."

Several years went by and we decided to move to a bigger house to accommodate the size of our household. Shortly after that, my Grandmother passed away in our home.

More transition came. Happily, my Dad met a really nice lady whom he cared about and she cared as much for him. After dating for about eight months, they decided to get married. My Dad moved to her home in Washington, D.C.

My sons had grown very close to their Grand pop. He was always teaching them, playing with them, and telling them funny stories.

It was during that time in my life that I began to think, 'I want to go to college." I had not attended college after high school. I wanted to become a nurse, since I felt I was so naturally suited to the caring profession. I knew that I needed to step up to the plate to become an advocate for myself and my family. I began to reach out to the community in which I lived in. I became a passionate community resource connector. I continued in school, as well as working in my sons' classrooms and doing volunteer work in a hospital.

After a difficult year of Biology, Anatomy and Physiology, and a few other challenging classes, I made the decision to change my major to Psychology. I wanted to become a Social Worker and eventually a school counselor.

After going to school for 4 years, I graduated with an AA degree in Psychology. By this time, it was 1995. I started to attend a university to pursue my Bachelor's degree in Social Work; however, with financial needs of life and growing sons, I had to go to work full time. I was working, going to school, and caring for active teens. I never got to sit in one place very long.

In 1999, I had to drop out of stop school. I was on call many nights. It was during this time, that I sought counseling for our family. I really felt like I was coming apart at the seams.

Then came September 11, 2001, a day that changed many lives. My life took a major turn and a journey began that was life changing.

Fast forward to 2010, I had the pleasure of meeting J Dianne Tribble and Life Coaching. Several years later, and after a very difficult period of time in my life, I decided to become a Certified Christian Life Coach. I accomplished this in August 2013.

After going thru the certification to become a Life Coach, I felt I had something that would shape the rest of my life. I have a passion, actually, it is my Life Mission statement to "Dispel the stigma of mental illness in society."

I am now living my life with God completely in control and I listen for Him to lead me. He places people in my path who either "opens or close doors." I am on the best journey with the best tour guide and that is Jesus. His work leads me and guides me every single day of my life. I would not choose to live a day without being thankful   and   grateful   for   His   healing   love and forgiveness. I know that He died on a cross to cover all of the sins that I committed in my life. I am grateful. He has placed people in my life at just the right times.

I have been a nanny to several. I was a case manager for young adults in foster care who were transitioning into adult services. I was a supported living coordinator for developmentally disabled adults. I assisted 21 individuals with the care plans for their lives and supervised their home staff.

The skills I bring to the table are as diverse as the years I have been alive. The skills that I have, that I feel God has equipped me with, are as follows: networker, connector, nurturer, listener, mentor, creativity, discerning spirit, and the ability to come up with creative solutions to whatever is handed to me.

Your past hurts may have left scars on you, but, don't wear them as a badge. Live each day with joy.

~ Coach Cindy Coates

Meditation Moment with Coach Cindy

God says join me and I will bless you in the Godly things you do.

Do you live as if you believe in God?

God lives in the presence of his people.

Praise unlocks God's power in your life.

God is at work for you and in you.

I wish peace for you today, I wish happiness for you today. Take time to look at something from a different perspective. Look at the sky, the clouds, the trees, a bird, a tree, or person. Think about what these things or that person means to you today at this very moment. Don't live waiting for greater moments in time. This is the moment that you can choose to really begin living. **~ Coach Cindy Coates**

The Heart of Coaching

By Coach Cindy Coates

The heart of coaching lies within the Coach and Client relationship. We want to see people as God sees them. God has been working in the life of a Client long before the Client and Coach connect. Clients are prompted to act on their plans by the Holy Spirit which dwells within them.

A Coach's job is to support, encourage, and hold the person accountable. Coaching is all about laying groundwork, establishing trust, building a relationship, clarifying expectations, and setting goals.

Coaches guide the process by listening and asking

exploratory questions. Exploratory questions are open ended questions which invite discussion. They are the best questions to ask in Coaching.

Our goal as listeners is to Reframe, Rephrase and Restate questions in a way that will cause the Client to engage fully in the problem solving process. Ownership must always be placed back on the person being coached.

Sometimes people are stuck in ways that are not healthy. This is when we can encourage and inspire them through scriptures. We should avoid offering direct solutions to problems. The Client will be more motivated to make changes if he or she knows the idea was generated from his or her own thought process. The Client drives the agenda. The process is not about the Coach. The Coach is simply there to guide the Client and facilitate the creative thinking process.

Taking a Spiritual Inventory

*How is my relationship with others?

*Who am I holding a grudge against?

*Am I seeking revenge for something?

*Am I jealous?

*Who have I been critical of or gossiped about?

*Am I serving God or serving man?

*Do I have an attitude of gratitude?

*Am I humble and non-judgmental?

I must look in the mirror and see myself as others see me. Let me always look at others thru the eyes of Jesus.

People see our priorities by our actions.

~ Coach Cindy Coates

Reflective Thoughts

_____

_____

_____

Anger Management

"Do not let the sun go down while you are still angry." `~ Ephesians 4:26

Types of Anger

Anger Avoidance-Non confrontational-it doesn't roll off your back; it gets stuck.

Passive Aggressive- the person does not let you know they are mad, they get even.

Sudden Anger- blow-up and walk away.

Planned Anger - take power and manipulate (i.e. bullying).

Addictive Anger - enjoys the adrenaline rush that comes with anger.

You will never be truly free in your thought life until you have forgiven people who have hurt you. Even if they don't know, don't care, or don't deserve it, forgive. Don't poison your mind with the negativity of un-forgiveness. It is toxic to your soul and spirit. Take one Day at a time. You don't have to do it all today. You just have to do today, today.

~ Coach Cindy Coates

I capture the moooving moments of your life.
~ Coach Cindy Coates

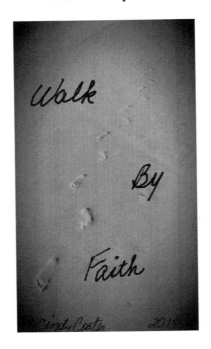

Coach Cindy Coates Contact Information
Cindy Coates, CPCLC
Business Name: Coates Creative Coaching
Business Line: (904) 434-2904
Email Address: CoachCoatesConnects@gmail.com
Face Book: www.Facebook.com/womenandvisionsempowered
Mailing address: 7234 Bonneval Road. Jacksonville, FL 32256

My Favorites

Scripture
"A friend loves at all times, and a brother is born for a time of adversity."

Proverbs 17:17

Quote
"Let everything be obliterated if it doesn't begin with God. Pick up the mantle of leadership."
~ UNKNOWN

Poem
"Trees"
By Joyce Kilmer

Personal Quote
"Photographs are memories recorded forever in the album of life."
~ Coach Cindy Coates

~ Coach Cindy Coates

At the Table Core Competencies

To experience the highest level of success and effectiveness as a Life Coach, the following core competencies should play active roles in the Coaching process.

- ❖ Secure the coaching relationship
- ❖ Establish the coaching guidelines and contract
- ❖ Establish the safe environment
- ❖ Exercise active listening
- ❖ Ask probing questions
- ❖ Exploration
- ❖ Execution planning
- ❖ Support
- ❖ Evaluating

- ❖ **Secure the coaching relationship** – This consists of the initial meet & greet or introduction to the potential new Client. This may be face-to-face or by phone. The Coach finds out what brings the potential Client to Coaching. During this initial meeting, the Client and Coach get to know a bit about each other. The Coach ensures the potential Client has an accurate understanding of Life Coaching.

- ❖ **Establish the coaching guidelines and contract** – At this point, the Client has agreed to enter into a coaching relationship with the Coach. The Coach and Client agree upon coaching terms. Expectations are clearly made known. The contract is signed by both parties.

- ❖ **Establish the safe environment** – The Coach provides the assurance of privacy and confidentiality. The Coach shares life stories and possibly his or her testimony. Trust is being built.

- ❖ **Exercise active listening** – The Client should dominate at least 80% of the dialogue during the training sessions. The Coach exercises intuitive listening skills. "W.A.I.T. (Why am I talking)."

- ❖ **Ask probing questions** – The Coach guides the coaching process through both intuitive listening and asking probing questions (direct, indirect, and ownership questions). The use of assessments may be used to determine what area the Client would like to focus on.

- ❖ **Exploration** –   The Client thinks through the process and considers alternatives. Bigger or deeper probing question are asked by the Coach. The "ah ha" moments are birthed and explored.

- ❖ **Execution planning** – The Client sets action steps to accomplish prior to following session. The Client sets goals.

- ❖ **Support** – The Coach provides the support the Client needs in order to stay on track and to successfully complete each goal. The Coach also encourages the Client when unexpected outcomes or setbacks occur. The Coach helps the Client to resist giving up.

- ❖ **Evaluating** – The Coach holds the Client accountable by asking for a status on action steps at the beginning of each session. The Client and Coach also should do periodic checks to determine whether the Coaching process is effective.

Resolutions & Goal Setting

As each year draws to a close, the word "resolution" becomes the buzz word of the hour. People all around the world begin to entertain areas in their lives in which they would like to change or need to change. You commonly hear resolutions like, "I'm going to lose weight. I'm going to stop drinking or smoking. I'm going back to school. I'm going to get organized," to name just a few. I'm sure we would agree that these sound good and would promote health and well-being. "So what's the problem?" you may ask.

While each of these resolutions sound good, on average, they never come to fruition. "Why is this so?" you may ask. It is because they lack the accountability required in order to be accomplished. Without the accountability, each resolution is no more than a good or bright idea, fleeting thought, or idle chatter.

Have you noticed how resolutions are often forgotten about before the end of the first quarter of each year? When the resolution was made, the intention was to see it come to pass. Maybe the person could actually see himself/herself walking victoriously in the desired outcome. What prevented the resolution from coming to pass?

The missing element was "structure" or "boundaries." To explain, when an area is identified as an area of improvement or change, it is imperative to set goals in order to produce the desired outcome. Each goal must have a projected end date. The end date supplies the energy required to achieve the goal.

Putting the goal in writing also increases the likelihood of the goal coming to pass. It provided an extra measure of accountability. Giving up or quitting on the goal becomes more unlikely.

When setting goals, consider the following:

1. **Exactly what would I like to accomplish.** It is important to clearly define what you want. This area may start off broad. If so, work on either narrowing the goal down or tackle it in manageable "chunks." Set action steps.

2. **How will you know when you've reached the goal?** Consider this on the front-end (i.e. if you set a goal to walk two miles a day, how will you know or what can you do to alert you that you've walked the two miles?)

3. **When would you like to see the goal completed?** Set a realistic date.

Even if you follow the suggested steps, there are times when your best efforts do not produce desired results. If this is the case, go back and revisit your goals and make any adjustments necessary in order to complete them. Resist the spirit of discouragement!

Soliciting the help of a Life Coach in reaching goals may be another option for you. Goal setting plays an important role in Life Coaching. A professional Life Coach provides the support and accountability a Client needs in order to reach his/her goals.

On the following page, consider what you would like to accomplish in the next 30 days, six months, and one year.

My Projected Goals

30 Day Goals

1._____
2._____
3._____
4._____
5._____

Six Months Goals

1._____
2._____
3._____
4._____
5._____

One Year Goals

1._____
2._____
3._____
4._____
5._____

Signature: _____ **Date:** _____

Resist the urge to give up. Keep working it. Payday is coming. You will surely reap if you faint not. Surround yourself with some positive, encouraging people. Don't allow yourself to get stuck in a rut. Cheering you on! You can do it. You can do it! ~ Coach J Dianne Tribble

There is a timing associated with everything that has your name on it. ~ Coach J Dianne Tribble

Is this your time to consider becoming a Certified Professional Life Coach?

Ecclesiastes 3: 1-8

"To everything there is a season, and a time to every purpose under the heaven: A time to be born, and a time to die; a time to plant, and a time to pluck up that which is planted; A time to kill, and a time to heal; a time to break down, and a time to build up; A time to weep, and a time to laugh; a time to mourn, and a time to dance; A time to cast away stones, and a time to gather stones together; a time to embrace, and a time to refrain from embracing; A time to get, and a time to lose; a time to keep, and a time to cast away; A time to rend, and a time to sew; a time to keep silence, and a time to speak; A time to love, and a time to hate; a time of war, and a time of peace."

Seasons

We can't get around them. We must go through them.

There will be times when things are all but perfect. Enjoy them and maximize those times.

There will be times of storms. Turn the wipers on and keep the umbrella handy. Suit up and go through.

There will be times when there are so many demands on you and it will seem like everyone wants a portion of your time. Get proper rest, take a deep breath, and prioritize. Do what you should. Do what you can. If your name's not on it, let it go.

There will also be the quiet and slow times. These can come as blessings in disguise. Use them wisely. Sit down. Catch up on tasks. Catch up on your reading and research. When things are quiet and slow, focus on listening. Avoid jamming the season with your own noise.

~ Coach J Dianne Tribble

Identifying Purpose

Have you ever had a desire and longing to do something and just couldn't shake it? That's one way of identifying your purpose in life. You talk about it. You constantly think about it. You literally dream about it. It just will not go away. So what do you do? Start entertaining it. Start praying about it. Identify others who will support your dream. We all need someone to talk to and to share our ideas with. Follow your heart and take steps toward realizing your dream. Support others' dreams and you will find it will reciprocate. Others will support you. Be careful of merging in another dreamer's lane! Follow the path set before you and in due time, you will find you are living your dream and great will be the rewards. Stay the course! Stay encouraged! Obtain the prize! Make a difference! Be another dreamer's example of success. You can do it! So get busy moving forward! ~ *Coach J Dianne Tribble*

Have you identified your purpose? _____
What is it? _____

Action Step:
What steps are you willing to take after reading this book to move to towards or forward in fulfilling your purpose?
1. _____
2. _____
3. _____

You Are Special

"I praise you because I am fearfully and wonderfully made;
your works are wonderful,
I know that full well" ~ Psalms 139:14

Epilogue

We trust you have enjoyed our stories and the various content we have shared from our hearts. This project was birthed from our passion to see people "unstuck" and winning at life. That passion includes you! Now, what are you motivated to do with what has been shared? Could this be the ideal time to commit to becoming a certified professional Life Coach? Would you like to explore the process with a professional representative?

At the Table Life Coaching & Motivational Speaking Services LLC offers an excellent, highly sought after professional Christian Life Coach Certification program. Through this program, you will learn the skills and techniques, which drive high-yielding results in assisting others.

One of the greatest benefits of the program, is the fact that each new Trainee and new Life Coach becomes a part of a coaching community. This uniquely sets our program apart from many others. In other words, at At the Table, we do not certify Life Coaches and send them off on their own to figure out how to work "it." As strong believers in life-long learning, we provide on-going training each quarter, special events, and fellowship opportunities. We support the success of each other. No one Life Coach can meet the needs of everyone or be the best fit for everyone. When we help others, we believe, we also help ourselves. It's all about "group elevation."

We would like to share more details with you. Take the step today to make the call or access the website to set things in motion.

At the Table Life Coaching & Motivational Speaking Services LLC

Business Line: (904) 613-8437

Email: **coaching@atthetableinc.com**

Website: **www.atthetableinc.com** (Please complete the "Contact Us" form. We will respond promptly in 24-48 hours).

First Quarter 2015 Coaches At the Table Workshop participants.

We look forward to you joining us "At the Table" soon.

Here's to your continuous success!

~ Coach J Dianne Tribble

Most Requested Workshops offered At the Table

- ❖ **The Essential "C" Experience**

- ❖ **Taking the Plunge**

- ❖ **Funnel Vision**

- ❖ **The Star Inside of You**

- ❖ **The Write Stuff: Journaling the Journey**

To Contact Coach J Dianne Tribble:
For At the Table Life Coaching & Motivational Speaking
Services, book signings, and speaking engagements:
Business Line: (904) 613-8437
Website: www.atthetableinc.com
Email: coaching@atthetableinc.com

Picture Gallery

Coaches/ Authors from Left to Right: Iris T. Moore, Cindy Coates, Gigi Blackshear, Gina Jackson, J Dianne Tribble, Ronline Cannady, & Alvin W. King

Fun At the Table

Coaches At the Table Christmas Party 2014. This is a picture of just a few of the attendants. We had a ball!

Anthology Authors' Directory

Coach Gigi Blackshear   (904) 239-2320

Coach Ronline Cannady   (904) 357-0840

Coach Cindy Coates   (904) 434-2904

Coach Gina Jackson   (904) 833-5210

Coach Alvin W. King   (904) 515-WIN (2946)

Coach Shara Mondy   (904) 333-3555

Coach Iris T. Moore   (904) 651-4344

Coach J Dianne Tribble   (904) 613-8437

It's time to remove the masks, connect the dots, and

fill in the blanks.

Your question marks will become periods.

It's time to unveil your full potential.

Are you ready?

We trust you have enjoyed our stories and will greatly benefit from the various tools found within the book. We believe in you! Let us hear from you soon. We are here to provide personal Life Coaching services, as well as to prepare those interested, in next steps in becoming Certified Professional Christian Life Coaches.

~ Coach J Dianne Tribble

(904) 613-8437 **www.atthetableinc.com**

Email: coaching@atthetableinc.com

At the Table
Life Coaching & Motivational Speaking Services
Unveiling Your Full Potential

In a day and age when life presents so many challenges, we are here to assist our clients in successfully coping, embracing change, and living life to their full potential.

Let's identify it; deal with it; and get ready to soar!
~ Coach J Dianne Tribble

www.atthetableinc.com

Business Line: (904) 613-8437

Made in the USA
Charleston, SC
24 January 2015